KCM

PERFORMING A CHRISTIAN LIFE

God and the Good Life

Thomas D. Kennedy

Performing a Christian Life:
God and the Good Life

A Timely, Theologically Rich Exploration of *What it Means to Live a Christian Life*

In his new book, *Performing a Christian Life*, Thomas D. Kennedy, Professor of Philosophy and Dean of the Evans School of Humanities, Arts and Social Sciences at Berry College, doesn't shy away from the tough questions: "You and I and all of our friends have at least this in common: we want to live well. We want to live good lives, whatever that means. And that's the problem—what does it mean? What is a good life? What does it mean to live well? Is the answer the same for all of us? How should those who understand themselves to be followers of Jesus (not to mention rational beings) understand living well? In short, how should one understand and perform a Christian life in light of one's understanding of God and the good?"

One of the reasons that Kennedy, a professor of Philosophy and Dean of the Evans School of Humanities, Arts and Social Sciences at Berry College, wrote *Performing a Christian Life* was his concern about how hard it is to know who one *really* is, and to remember who one is in our everyday lives. "Daily we are barraged with information and media that not only distract us from the things that matter but also tear us away from our deepest identities," said Kennedy.

Kennedy draws upon his deep knowledge of western philosophical and theological traditions to help readers

Suggested Interview Questions for

Thomas D. Kennedy

➤ Why is it important for Christians examine what it means to live well?

➤ When someone is "morally lost" can they be "morally found"?

➤ Talk about projects – what is the importance of being able to identify "ground" projects from among ordinary or common ones?

➤ Why would a good God permit horrendous evils? How does a Christian justify that?

➤ Is the awareness of evil in the world necessarily a motivation to do good? Instead, could it lead to moral paralysis?

➤ What makes a prayer a *good* prayer? How might prayer make a difference for Christian living, for following Jesus?

➤ In the book, you discuss that a cornerstone of Dr. Martin Luther

Thomas D. Kennedy

Thomas D. Kennedy is Professor of Philosophy and Dean of the Evans School of Humanities, Arts and Social Sciences at Berry College in

Mount Berry, Georgia. Coeditor of *From Christ to the World: Introductory Readings in Christian Ethics*, he has written and taught widely in ethics, both theoretical and practical, and Philosophical theology.

https://www.tomdkennedy.com/

https://www.facebook.com/Performing-a-Christian-Life-God-and-the-Good-Life-102732871204808/

King Jr.'s civil rights work was his belief in the dignity of all human beings, and his conviction that certain things are right and wrong independent of whether we believe them to be right and wrong, beliefs that were based on his beliefs about God and God's story. Could one/should one have as strong a commitment to protecting the dignity of all human beings without a belief in God?

➤ What elements are essential to a life of virtue? How does Pope Francis arrive at the belief that "the vocation to be protectors" of God's creation is "essential" to a life of virtue?

➤ What is hypocrisy? Is there any upside to being a hypocrite?

➤ Talk about your assertion that "Without the singing of Christ and the harmony of the Holy Spirit, we could not now or in the future perform God's melody as we should."

Thomas D. Kennedy

Cascade/Wipf and Stock
Paperback - $23.00
ISBN: 9781532689897

Contact:
Judy McDonough
judy@karencampbellmedia.com

Karen Campbell
karen@karencampbellmedia.com

understand living a good life in light of who they are, and in light of their Christian identities. As a way to underscore the discussion in each chapter, Kennedy includes brief stories of influential Christians - including Augustine, Dietrich Bonhoeffer, Esther John, and Martin Luther King, Jr.) - whose lives or thoughts can help us better understand and live a good life.

Additionally, a set of questions is included at the end of each chapter; Kennedy encourages the reader to use the questions as a way to slow down and absorb the information, or to use them to instigate conversations with others as well.

By taking an honest, thoughtful look at the deep questions posed by *Performing a Christian Life*, Kennedy wants to share a most precious gift: "Christians are people of hope, and that hope is a gift we can bring to those around us. The world needs us to be hopeful. We can live good lives, even in very hard times. We see that in the lives of hope-filled Christians who have weathered storms before us. We see that in the lives of our living brothers and sisters who are *for* God and *for* the good despite the difficulties they daily face. The world needs us to perform our lives, to perform *God's* music of peace and justice, and to perform our lives hopefully."

PERFORMING A CHRISTIAN LIFE

God and the Good Life

THOMAS D. KENNEDY

CASCADE *Books* · Eugene, Oregon

PERFORMING A CHRISTIAN LIFE
God and the Good Life

Cascade Books
An Imprint of Wipf and Stock Publishers
199 W. 8th Ave., Suite 3
Eugene, OR 97401

www.wipfandstock.com

PAPERBACK ISBN: 978-1-5326-8971-0
HARDCOVER ISBN: 978-1-5326-8972-7
EBOOK ISBN: 978-1-5326-8973-4

Cataloguing-in-Publication data:

Names: Kennedy, Thomas D., 1955–, author.

Title: Performing a Christian life : God and the good life / by Thomas D. Kennedy.

Description: Eugene, OR : Cascade Books, 2019 | Includes bibliographical references and index.

Identifiers: ISBN 978-1-5326-8971-0 (paperback) | ISBN 978-1-5326-8972-7 (hardcover) | ISBN 978-1-5326-8973-4 (ebook)

Subjects: LCSH: Christian ethics. | Christian life. | Happiness—Religious aspects—Christianity.

Classification: BJ1251 .K38 2019 (paperback) | BJ1251 .K38 (ebook)

Manufactured in the U.S.A.   11/11/19

Scripture quotations are from New Revised Standard Version Bible, copyright © 1989 National Council of the Churches of Christ in the United States of America. Used by permission. All rights reserved worldwide.

In chapter 1, "The Road Ahead" from "The Love of Solitude" from THOUGHTS IN SOLITUDE by Thomas Merton. Copyright © 1958 by the Abbey of Our Lady of Gethsemani. Copyright renewed 1986 by the Trustees of the Thomas Merton Legacy Trust. Reprinted by permission of Farrar, Straus and Giroux.

In chapter 4, permission to use some revised material from my essay "Habit's Harsh Bondage" has been granted by Baylor University.

In chapter 9, permission to use the Erik Routley translation of the Imre text for "There in God's Garden" has been granted by Hope Publishing Company.

PERFORMING A CHRISTIAN LIFE

For Agnes and Emmanuel

Taste and see that the LORD is good.

—Psalm 34:8

The road to the promised land runs past Sinai.

—C. S. Lewis, *The Problem of Pain*

CONTENTS

ACKNOWLEDGMENTS

In a book with a history as long as this one, debts are many—and many, perhaps most, of these debts I've forgotten. Many of us developed our first significant ground projects in conversations with teachers and mentors and friends in small college settings. In some sense, this book began when I stumbled upon Rich Mouw's *Political Evangelism* in the bookstore of a small college in South Carolina long ago. *Political Evangelism* and Rich Mouw led me to Calvin College, and that, in one way and another, has made much of the difference. Rich and Nick Wolterstorff have been teachers, friends, and models of engaged Christian scholarship for most of my life. I'm grateful to have had their lead to follow as I journey "in this world of wonders."[1] Nick and Rich may wish my debt to them deeper, or at least more apparent, but what a wonderful debt it is. My indebtedness to John Rottman, a friend since those early student days with Rich and Nick, is much different, but no less wonderful, than what I owe to Rich and Nick.

More directly, this book began in conversations with two Hope College colleagues who were as good of colleagues as one could hope for anywhere, at any time, Allen Verhey and Wayne Boulton, both of whom have passed too soon. After our edited volume, *From Christ to the World: Introductory Readings in Christian Ethics*, was published, I began discussing this project with them, and then with our editor at Wm. B. Eerdmans, Jon Pott, all of whom were enthusiastic. Allen and Wayne were the best of mentors and friends, remaining so for years after we had gone our separate ways. They believed in this work, or something like it. The same can be said of Gilbert Meilaender, especially if we emphasize "or something like it." Valparaiso University and a generous grant from the Louisville Institute supported

---

1. Wolterstorff, *World of Wonders*, 317.

some early work on parts of what became this project. Gil was generous in reading and commenting on some of that early work.

More recently, Berry College student Blake Trenary and Berry faculty colleagues Andrea Hollingsworth, Jonathan Parker, Jonathan Huggins, and Marshall Jenkins have carefully read and commented on some or all of the manuscript. The book is better for their interest and their comments. Kathy B. Richardson, former provost at Berry and now president of Westminster College, PA, has been a good friend and was supportive and helpful as Berry College provided me a sabbatical in which to pull things together. Diane Land has provided extraordinary assistance in readying this manuscript.

My family, like my teachers, and like my friends, has shared with me many of the goods of my life. I owe so much in so many ways to Melodie and our children: our daughter, Kate, her husband, Joel, and our son, Ian. As always, and in all things, I owe the most to Melodie, who has long journeyed with me. It has been good not to be alone, and especially good to wander and wonder with her. She read and commented on the entire manuscript (and her comments were perhaps less perfunctory than I had hoped). True to her self-giving nature, she would rather that the book be dedicated to our beautiful grandchildren, Agnes and Emmanuel, than to her. And so it is.

INTRODUCTION

Y ou and I and all of our friends have at least this in common: we want
to live well. We want to live good lives, whatever that means. And that's
the problem—what does it mean? What is a good life? What does it mean
to live well? Life can be good in lots of different ways. You can have a good
job, a good marriage, a good dog, and a good three-point shot. You can have
one or two of these and still feel that you are not living well. And sometimes
it seems like there are as many views about what a good life is as there are
people. "He who dies with the most toys wins" has been a tempting view
of the good life for many Americans. But, really? Even if we look only at
Americans, the most consumerist people on earth, few of us really believe
that wealth and the consumption of stuff that riches allow is the only thing,
or even the largest thing that matters for living well. According to a recent
index of the Charities Aid Foundation, Americans are among the most generous people.[2] We buy a lot of stuff, and we give a lot of money away. Having
lots of money and lots of stuff is not all that matters to us. After all, as the
bumper sticker says, "He who dies with the most toys . . . still dies." Toys do
matter to most of us; so does death.

But what *should* matter to us? And how much should these various
things matter to us? Again, most of us agree on at least some problematic
answers to this question. Former Harvard philosopher John Rawls asks us
to imagine a person whose only pleasure in life is to count blades of grass in
places like park squares and lawns. Could that be a good life for a rational
person? What if, instead, a person devoted herself to sitting in front of a
television for at least ten hours a day, every day, with an open bag of Cheetos
in front of her to see how many days in a row she could go without eating a

---

2. Charities Aid Foundation, "CAF World Giving Index 2018."

single Cheeto? Could that be a well-lived life? Most of us don't think so, but why? How do we know this?

The ancient philosopher Aristotle thought a good starting place for figuring out what really matters for living well is to ask people we respect, people we think are smart about such things, what they think. He thought wise people would all pretty much agree on what makes for a good life, as well as what makes for a not so good life. We understand ourselves to be rational creatures, Aristotle argued; so, to live well, to live a good life, is to live a life in which you exercise your reason in the right sorts of ways—you make choices and pursue good things the way a rational person would.

But Aristotle recognized that living well is not just a matter of one's choices, not just a matter of what one *does*, but is also a matter of what happens to us. Things may go badly for us, and this will at least diminish the goodness of our lives, and maybe make living well impossible for us. And things may go badly for us in almost as many ways as things may go well. We marry the wrong person, or we take the wrong job, or we look at our phone at the wrong time. But that is still, at least to some significant extent, a matter of what we *do*, what we choose. As Aristotle notes, fortune, or luck, also matters a lot for how well our lives go. The absence of certain things in our life—good birth, good children, beauty (and we could add other things like health, and at least a minimal level of intelligence)—"mars our blessedness."[3] A good life *is* a blessed life, and some lives seem more blessed than others, through no apparent fault of anyone.

Aristotle, of course, was not alone among the ancients in affirming the connection between a good life and a blessed life, between living well and living blessedly. Some three hundred years later, Jesus of Nazareth preached these words: "Blessed are the poor in spirit . . . Blessed are those who mourn . . . Blessed are the meek . . . Blessed are those who hunger and thirst for righteousness . . . Blessed are the merciful . . . Blessed are the pure in heart . . . Blessed are the peacemakers . . ." He continues with words most of us prefer to forget: "I say to you, love your enemies and pray for those who persecute you, so that you may be children of your Father in heaven" (Matt 5:3–10, 43–45; Luke 6:20–36 NRSV).

Although Jesus connects a good life with blessedness, there's no doubt that he understands the good life much differently than Aristotle, and that both understand the good life and living well much differently than the current president of the United States, Donald Trump, and probably differently than most Americans. What makes a life a good life? What does it mean to live well? Is the answer the same for all of us? How should those who

---

3. Aristotle, *Nicomachean Ethics*, 1099b.

understand themselves to be followers of Jesus (not to mention rational beings) understand living well? In short, how should one understand and perform a Christian life in light of one's understanding of God and the good?
That is the question of this book.

In chapter 1, we'll try to get a better sense of where you and I and most
of the people we know really are when it comes to living well. I'll argue
that questions about the good life and the moral life are very difficult (and
although the moral life is not identical with the good life, I'll assume that
part of what it means to live well is to live morally, to care about what we
owe to others and about being certain sorts of people). Most of us are lost
in answering these questions about living a good life, although we may not
realize it. Most of us live in a world that distracts us from thinking about
where we are going in our lives, that diverts our attention from the things
that matter most for living well. As Socrates thought, recognizing that one
is lost, that one doesn't really know what one thinks one knows, is a crucial
first step in living well.

Another early step is trying to understand oneself. In the opening of
his *Institutes of the Christian Religion*, the great Reformation theologian
John Calvin wrote that true wisdom has two parts, knowing God *and* knowing ourselves, the second part dependent upon the first. In chapter 2, we
try to make some progress in understanding ourselves, in grasping what it
means to be a person, to have an identity. One thing that is required for being somebody is having a coherent story of oneself, a narrative that connects
the pieces of one's life.

But, of course, people have different understandings of themselves and
tell different stories about who they are—if they even have (and even if they
have) personal narratives. We Americans, and perhaps others, live in a place
and time that discourages us from being still, from paying attention to our
lives, and from understanding ourselves. Beginning in chapter 3, we explore
the story that Christians, followers of Jesus, tell about the world and what
they think that story means for their own story. Christians understand their
own story as part of a bigger story, as part of God's story, and because of that,
as connected to the stories of other Christians. No one stands alone.

Many Christian theologians have argued that all Christians must un-
dergo two conversions. The first conversion is a turning away from sin, from
loving the wrong things, and from loving the right things in wrong ways.
Jesus calls us to repent and, repenting, to follow him. When we follow Jesus,
we follow him back to the world, back to God's rich and wonderful creation,
groaning as it awaits its transformation, as it is becoming a new creation
(Rom 8:19–23). In chapters 5–7, we try to think about God and what understanding God rightly means for making sense of goodness and values and

what matters for living well. We consider who God is, God's character, and the projects God undertakes in creating the universe God has created, and what all that means for who we should try to be and how we should go about understanding and living a good life. Finally, we consider human nature, our own loves, cares, and projects, and the implications of God's project for understanding who we are and who we may wish to become.

In chapter 8, we turn to Christian calling, the *vocation* of Christians, and identify the sense in which living a good life is the vocation of Christians, even those Christians whose circumstances in life make the pursuit of basic human goods, the things that normally make a life a good life, most challenging. The vocation of Christians is to be *for* the goods that God has created and to pursue these goods with others, the church. To live, with others, a life *for* God and *for* the goods is to live well, despite the many hurdles and hardships that we may face.

In each chapter, I include some brief information about a Christian, often a Christian philosopher or theologian, whose life and thought illuminate the discussion. Christians recognize these as our brothers and sisters in a body of Christ that spans the centuries. It is good to meet them and to learn from them. Our brothers and sisters, even when they are, or were, more virtuous than we are, were not perfect, as we are not perfect. Still, we sing together.

We conclude with a musical meditation, a reflection upon living the good life as like performing music, a song we sing, and play, with others. How can we keep from singing, given God's story, and ours? How can we keep from playing, having seen the Tree of Life?

Easter, 2019

I

LOST

Whether you think of yourself as a "none" or "spiritual but not religious" or as a Christian of some sort or as something else—and maybe you're not sure—you've heard the claims. Spirituality and Jesus are okay. But religion, especially organized Christianity? Not so much. Organized or institutional religion (that is, the folks who self-identify as Christian and who meet together on Sunday morning in some kind of church) is harsh and judgmental. Here's a typical account:

> For me (and probably most of us) there was a giant disconnect between the character of Jesus and then the way his followers demanded you live. *I liked Jesus.* He seemed kind and compassionate and enjoyed associating with the people I associated with (the party crowd). However, I wasn't interested in being a "Christian" if it meant looking like the status quo. His people were moral Nazis, and they had really strange rules.[1]

Initially, this *Jesus is cool but Christianity is narrow-minded and harsh and judgmental* view might surprise those who are most familiar with the Christian Scriptures. After all, if you read the Bible, even if you start with what Christians call the New Testament, Jesus, despite his fondness for sheep and his care for children, appears not to be as chill as we are usually inclined to think. He sometimes loses his temper (see the story of Jesus and the money changers in Matt 21:12–17), and he is sometimes very

1. Sledge, "Why I'm a Christian," para. 8. A similar expression can be found in Matson, "I'm Ashamed": https://sojo.net/articles/im-ashamed-christianity-never-christ.

judgmental (see his criticism of the Pharisees in Luke 11:37–54). And he keeps demanding that those who hear him should, as he says, "Repent!"

Admittedly, we can read him as being critical of the religious establishment, of the first-century Jewish analogue to Christianity. And rightly so, we may think. But his judgment ranged considerably further. Here are some things Jesus said, hard things that today's organized Christianity appears much less judgmental and much more lenient about than gentle Jesus:

- "Whoever divorces his wife and marries another commits adultery against her; and if she divorces her husband and marries another, she commits adultery." (Mark 10:10–12; Matt 5:27–32; Luke 16:18)

- "Whoever comes to me and does not hate father and mother, wife and children, brothers and sisters, yes, and even life itself, cannot be my disciple." (Luke 14:26; Matt 10:37)

- "Be perfect, therefore, as your Heavenly Father is perfect." (Matt 5:48)

- "Go, sell what you own, and give the money to the poor, and you will have treasure in heaven; then come, follow me." (Mark 10:21–22; Luke 18:22; Matt 19:21)

- "You have heard that it was said, 'An eye for an eye and a tooth for a tooth.' But I say to you, Do not resist an evildoer. But if anyone strikes you on the right cheek, turn the other also; and if anyone wants to sue you and take your coat, give your cloak as well; and if anyone forces you to go one mile, go also the second mile. Give to everyone who begs from you, and do not refuse anyone who wants to borrow from you." (Matt 5:38–42)

In each of these cases Jesus *is* judgmental and his words are harsh. In none of these cases do many (if any) of today's churches follow Jesus' hard words. We may be (we certainly ought to be) reluctant to describe Jesus as a moral Nazi. (We ought to be wary anytime someone pulls out the Nazi card, trivializing, as it usually does, the horrendous moral atrocities of the Nazis). But, in comparison to Jesus' radical moral teaching, we ought to describe the organized Christian church as a bunch of moral wusses. Maybe Jesus isn't quite the nice guy we tend to think he is? Maybe the church isn't quite as bad as we've been thinking? Or maybe the church is as bad as we've been thinking, but not quite in the way in which we've been thinking.

But that isn't how most of us—"nones," "spiritual but not religious," "post-Christian," or perhaps even religious, even Christian—usually think about these things. Why not? Does Jesus simply have a better public relations operation than Christianity and the Christian church? Are we constantly re-creating Jesus in our own image and for our own purposes?

I suspect the answer lies elsewhere. When it comes to how we should live and, in particular, to morality, to questions about what we owe to others and whether there are right and wrong or better and worse ways to live, most of us are more than a little bit confused. That's because morality itself, and not just religious morality or Christian morality, is pretty puzzling for everybody—atheist or spiritual person or religious or Christian or none of the above. When it comes to the good life and morality as a major compo-nent of a good life, once you start thinking carefully about it, you quickly discover that you are in some strange place and that you can't easily find your way around. You find that you are lost. We know that we have strong feelings about some things related to good and evil (or at least to justice and rights), and we tend to trust those strong feelings. What else is there, really, we think, other than our feelings? We know what we like and what we don't like. And we know we don't like a bunch of folks judging us and telling us what to do and what not to do, telling us whether we are good or bad people. We are different from them and they should leave us alone. Worse yet, those judgmental folks, we think, are hypocritical. They seem not to be telling themselves to stop doing what *we* think is stupid and wrong. Usually, it seems to many of us that especially Christians and other religious folk, not Jesus, are the ones judging us, and we don't like that. But what if Jesus is right about how we should treat our enemies, that we should love them to the point of loss (and beyond), and the church and the rest of us are wrong? What if we really ought to sell all we have and give to the poor? And to always turn the other cheek? What if . . . ? But that couldn't be right, could it? That's pretty crazy! Who wants to live that way? Who could even figure out what it really means to live that way?

Knowing how we ought to live, what we should do and who we should be, is hard. Values are puzzling. Morality, as one type of value, is compli-cated and confusing, especially if Jesus is right about all those hard things he said and if his words are meant for us. Right and wrong, good and bad, should and should not—these abstract ideas can be pretty tough to grasp. It may be easy to feel things, but it is very hard to understand, to know how to think and what to believe about morality and about what we should do and how we should live. The things we should love and what we should and should not care about are not always easily grasped.

If you think I'm overcomplicating things, if you suspect that figuring out how to live well may not really be as hard and confusing as I've suggest-ed, if you think you and I are not just a bit more smug about our own moral goodness than we ought to be, consider punishment: what do we think, and what have you and I done (or not done), when it comes to punishment imposed by our state or nation on our behalf? We probably have thought about it very little and have done even less. Yet, implicitly, we have authorized the state to imprison individuals (and sometimes to kill them), among them folks guilty of drug offenses or sex offenses in which there is no victim, and no person has been harmed other than, perhaps, the offender. Sometimes we imprison offenders for years and we leave them with a record that will make it very difficult for them to find a job or ever to be productive citizens and equally hard for them to live well. Perhaps we all can agree that these offenders do deserve punishment, but why do we think a victimless crime deserves *this* punishment—imprisonment and a record that in some states may result in the loss of the right to vote? Mightn't it be much more just, much more fair, as criminologist Peter Moskos asks, to offer these guilty persons corporal punishment, such as flogging, rather than incarceration?[2]

What moral or criminal evil deserves what punishment? What wrongs may justify our interfering with a person's life in a way that severely diminishes the goodness of that life? Why are you and I so complacent (much more like the church and much less like Jesus) when it comes to caring for those in prison? Why our indifference to ministering to Jesus when we minister to the imprisoned, as Jesus suggested (Matt 25:36, 39)? Maybe our complacency is best explained by how complicated living well is and how complex morality is. Maybe it's because it can be pretty difficult to find our way through and about punishment and lots of other moral things. You don't have to be Christian, or even spiritual, to realize that we may have given ourselves a pass we don't deserve when it comes to how unconcerned we are about some of the ways our government acts on our behalf.

Or fails to act. Global climate change and its effects and what you and I should do to mitigate it is another difficult and confusing topic. What does it look like to live a good life knowing what we now know about global climate change? In reality, there is very little you or I *can* do that will have a real, significant impact on global climate change, so why should we bother? But what does it say about me if I don't care, if I don't bother?

But the difficult and confusing issues aren't just those big, "out there" social issues like punishment and global climate change. It's no less confusing to determine what I owe to my friends or what they owe to me, or how I should feel and how I should respond to my mother's dementia. What would a good friend or a good son feel and do? What do parents owe their own children in a world where many children are needy?

2. Moskos, *In Defense of Flogging*.

Trying to live well and be a good person is hard for all of us. Sometimes it's as though I've gone out onto the dance floor with my partner because we liked the rhythm of the song the DJ was playing—it's a piece that swings and we know how to swing. But then that song ends and the DJ immediately switches things up and moves to a different style of music that we are uncertain how to dance to. But we're out on the floor. What do we do? We look around, see what everyone else is doing, and pretty much do what they do until we can get off the floor. Maybe in the moment we realize that we are lost and the best solution seems to be to follow the crowd, to be a part of the herd. So, that's what we do. And maybe we are more lost than we realize. Maybe we forget or distract ourselves from thinking about how we felt on the dance floor the moment when the music changed.

Could it be that that's how it is for most of us most of the time when it comes to what we should care about, how we should feel, and how we should live—when it comes to morality and the moral life, to many of our deepest values? We're on the dance floor. We don't really know how to dance to this music we hear. But we can follow our crowd and try to do what everyone else seems to be doing and, probably, if we stay in the crowd, get through this dance, sooner or later. Is that how things really are with us?

1.1 THE HUMAN CONDITION?

Imagine yourself in an orchestra rehearsal. You start out playing along with everyone else—at least you think you started out with everyone else—but now, as you listen to the performers around you and notice the music of your own strings, you can hear that something isn't right. You look at your music only to discover that you've lost your place. What is everyone else playing? You look at the conductor but you still can't make out where you should be. You try to play along, but you cannot find a fit between the music you are making and the music of your peers and the lead of the conductor. Nothing seems to work. Nothing seems to help until the assistant conductor slides up beside you, replaces your score with a different score, and points to the line you should be playing. You play, again, harmoniously, no longer lost but found.

Now imagine that you are a university student. As you read your school newspaper you notice an ad offering to pay up to $10,000 for the "donation" of your egg (sperm doesn't command nearly so high a price) to a loving but infertile or non-fertile couple seeking to have a child. The only stipulations are that you must be reasonably attractive and that you must score well on an IQ test. Ten thousand dollars for little more than an hour or two of your time and no lasting physical consequences to your health! Still, you are somewhat uneasy about the offer. Perhaps it seems to you too much like selling your body. But why shouldn't you sell your body? Is there anything *wrong* with selling your body? What could be wrong with selling your body if the price were right? It is *yours*, isn't it? Mightn't it be okay to sell parts of your body, especially replaceable parts? How is "donating" your eggs any different than donating your hair? Why would anyone think this might be something you ought not to do? How could anyone *know* this was wrong? How would you tell? How do you begin to determine whether you should pursue this business opportunity? Again, you realize that you are lost. Where do you find some bearings by which to navigate this decision? Where do you look for a way through this dilemma? Where is a morning star to guide you, a conductor to show you your place?

Or imagine that you are the president of the United States of America, the world's greatest military power, on September 11, 2001. Terrorists have attacked the Twin Towers in New York City. You are a Christian, and you are the commander in chief of the military forces of your nation. What should you do in response to this terrorist attack that has harmed your own citizens and, arguably, threatens democracy the world over? Who, if anyone, should you attack? Could it be wrong to attack the terrorists? And if you may not attack, what should you do? Are there any moral limits to what you may do? Is there any moral way to fight terrorism? Or is it the case that all is fair in war, and this is war? Does it even make sense to speak of war and morality in the same breath? What difference, if any, should your identity as a Christian make for your decisions in a nation where there is a distinct separation of church and state?

Although these are contemporary problems, this belief that you could be lost and the sense that you are lost, that you don't know where you are or how to proceed, is not unique to us twenty-first-century humans. In most cultures, in most times, we can find some people a lot like us who care about important questions, about morality and other values, but who are confused and feel lost. Some of us recognize our confusion, how lost we are, relatively early in our lives, maybe in our teens. Sadly, others of us may become aware of this condition of being lost only upon our deathbeds.

The great nineteenth-century Russian novelist Leo Tolstoy tells the story of Ivan Ilych, a lawyer who gradually rises to ever-greater heights of social and professional standing until an apparently minor accident upends his life and slowly and painfully pulls him to his last breaths.[3] On his death-bed, for the first time in his life, he worries, "Maybe I did not live my life as I

---

3. Tolstoy, *Death of Ivan Ilych*, 152.

ought to have done." As his physical pain increases, so also does his realization that *he has not* lived his life well. He thinks he hasn't understood what is really good and important in life. Instead, he has loved reputation and has sought the appreciation of others too much. He has loved others, especially those closest to him, too little. His actions, all the things he has done with his life, were in pursuit of lesser goods, and now, aware that death is calling to him, he cannot make the necessary corrections in his life. How could he have lived such a lost and confused, such a foolish life? How could he not have known better and chosen better? Why couldn't he have understood better, loved better, and lived better?

This may be our condition as well, or so Tolstoy worried. Confusion and a feeling of lostness, of just not getting it, arguably is a universal feature of reflective human life. We humans find ourselves confused, lost, and with a need to discover our bearings in order to make sense of ourselves and make progress in life, in order to understand our lives and to feel content with our lives. Those of us with the leisure to think about how our lives are going wonder what to do and who to be, what kind of life is worth living and what goods are worth possessing, what an excellent person looks like, and why we should care about being good. We wonder about what is true and try to understand life and the world and all its complexities. We struggle to identify and love what is genuinely valuable. We don't find it easy to know what things are of enduring value and to love the things that last, the genuinely worthy things—if there are, in fact, such things. We act. After all, we are caught in the middle of the dance floor. Yet we worry that our actions are ineffective, inconsequential, or may even harm others. We are less sure of who we are and what we are doing and where we are going than we would like to be, at least if we are thoughtful about our lives. We find ourselves lost, and in this we have plenty of company, good company, whoever we are.

Dietrich Bonhoeffer (1906–45)

For the German Lutheran theologian and pastor Dietrich Bonhoeffer, 1939 was a tumultuous year, a year of feeling especially lost and at sea. Although his musical talents were great enough that his parents anticipated a musical career for Dietrich, already at the age of fourteen he felt called by God to be a pastor and theologian. As a young man he established himself as an able scholar. By the early 1930s he had served as a pastor in Barcelona, Spain, and had engaged in additional theological studies in the United States, after which he returned to Berlin to serve as both theology teacher and pastor. By this time, he had resolved some confusion he had felt about what it means to live as a Christian when it comes to violence. He had become convinced that the way of Christ is a nonviolent way and that all Christians ought to be pacifists; good Christians do not aim to do grievous harm to other persons.

But Adolf Hitler had become chancellor of Germany in early 1933 and the world had changed for Bonhoeffer, as it had for all German Christians, as it had for all Germans. Hitler changed the world. In response to the apparent ugliness and the evil of Nazism, Bonhoeffer worked with other German pastors to call the German church to notice and to resist the crimes of the Nazi government. By the mid-1930s Bonhoeffer had become a leader of the Confessing Church, the Protestant church of Germany that in 1934 had publicly declared, "We repudiate the false teaching that there are areas of our life in which we belong not to Jesus Christ but to other lords, areas in which we do not need justification and sanctification through him."[4] The Nazi government officially banned the Confessing Church soon after the Barmen Synod of May 1934. In 1935, Bonhoeffer became director of one of the seminaries of the banned church.

The Nazis continued to ratchet up their attacks on people, particularly Jews, in the mid to late thirties. By September 1937 the Nazi government had closed the seminary at which Bonhoeffer was teaching, and more than twenty of his students had been arrested and imprisoned. Bonhoeffer continued his work as the seminary went underground, operating secretly. But disillusioned by the weakness of the Confessing Church, and fearful that he might be drafted into military service, Bonhoeffer escaped to America. He accepted an invitation to lecture and teach in the United States and moved to New York City.

In less than a month he found himself lost, wondering whether he had made a mistake in leaving Germany. As he wrote to his friend, the theologian Reinhold Niebuhr, "Christians in Germany will face the terrible alternative of either willing the defeat of their nation in order that Christian civilization may survive, or willing the victory of their nation and thereby destroying our civilization."[5]

Bonhoeffer then did an about-face, leaving the United States and returning to Germany in 1939. Again, he found himself lost. Who was he? What was his true identity? What was God calling him to be and

---

4. "The Barmen Confession" (May 1934). Quoted in the editors' introduction to Dietrich Bonhoeffer, *Testament to Freedom*, 21. The translation is that of Geffrey B. Kelly and F. Burton Nelson, who note that theirs is a slightly modified version of the text as it appears in Arthur C. Cochrane, *The Church's Confession under Hitler*, 237–47.

5. Bonhoeffer, *Theological Education Underground, 1937–1940*, 210.

to do? Soon after his return he discovered an opportunity to join with others in trying to bring an end to Hitler's hateful rule. Bonhoeffer's brother-in-law, Hans von Dohnanyi, was part of a group of military leaders intent upon removing Hitler from power and ending the attack upon German citizens and the Nazi threat to other nations. He enlisted Dietrich as a civilian member of the group, and Bonhoeffer worked as a double agent for this group for four years, assisting in plans to smuggle Jews out of Germany and conveying to Allied contacts vital information about the German resistance to Hitler's government.

Bonhoeffer now believed that he had found his way and that the obedience to which God was calling him required him to act to end Hitler's reign of terror. On April 5, 1943, following several failed attempts to kill Hitler, Bonhoeffer was arrested on a charge of "subversion of the armed forces." After another assassination attempt a year later, the Nazis discovered files that implicated Bonhoeffer and his brother-in-law as part of a conspiracy to kill Hitler. He was moved to the concentration camp at Buchenwald, then to Flossenbürg, where he was hanged on April 9, 1945, shortly after conducting a morning worship service. Two weeks later, this concentration camp was liberated by Allied forces.

How should Bonhoeffer have thought through leaving the safety of America to return to Germany? Was Bonhoeffer really lost? Was the decision to return to his native land a good decision? How could he decide, how should he have decided, whether or not he should be part of the conspiracy to assassinate Hitler? Why, given his pacifism, could he come to think that killing Hitler was the right thing to do? Was he mistaken in his earlier commitment to nonviolence, or was this somehow an exceptional case? Was there some roadmap he could have used to help him find his way? What do Christians owe their leaders? How should we think about evil leaders and the use of violence against evil leaders?

1.2 VARIETIES OF LOSTNESS: BELIEVING WELL, MORALITY, AND LIVING WELL

There are lots of different ways in which one can be lost. I may not know my way to the nearest Krispy Kreme donut shop, or whether the donuts currently on offer are hot (the best!). Or I may not know my way around converting centigrade to Fahrenheit or how to tell whether a turtle is male or female. I may not know whether to believe that Aurora or Torin really loves me. I may not know whether it is ever okay for the government to separate children from their parents. I may be at a loss explaining why you should listen more to Bach than you listen to Taylor Swift. When it comes to what we should believe, what we should love, and what we should do, there are lots of different ways to be lost, and different degrees of lostness.

One area of life, in particular, about which we humans from one generation to the next often seem confused and adrift is the good life, living well, and what seems a major aspect of the good life—the moral life. How can we live well? What should we aim at in our lives? How do we choose the projects that will make our lives happy and meaningful? What should you and I want out of our lives? What kinds of things should we care about? What sort of people should we be, or at least try to become? What should we recognize as important and what as unimportant? What, if anything, should we think of as valuable enough to die for? Are there things it is always wrong to want or to do, things we must be very careful never to do? What kind of life do we want for our children? What kind of people do we want our children to be? What do we owe to our neighbors? What do we owe to others far away (in space or in time)?

These are tough questions—tough to understand and try to think one's way through—for these questions are different from so many other sorts of questions. If we want to know how much damage secondhand smoke can do to children, we know where to look and what kinds of questions to ask. But if we want to figure out what we should think about smoking cigarettes or weed, about whether and how smoking cigarettes or weed might or might not fit into a well-lived life, it's not nearly so clear how to proceed (especially if we are in a context in which the legality of smoking is not an issue).

In short, in this particular area of life—but, wait a minute, is this an *area* of life? If so, what exactly is this area? We might think that this area of life is distinguished from other areas by how important it is to us, by how we *care* about this area of life in a distinctive way. To be human, it might be argued, is to be *a caring creature*, to care about some things greatly and about other things not so much. But even if that is true, it needs some nuance or qualification. Other species appear to care about things, too, although the range of the things they care about certainly seems small compared to the range of human cares. Dogs care about food, and their young offspring, and their human friends, and sniffing around, but that pretty much covers it. Rare is the dog who cares about hot Krispy Kreme donuts, or whether LeBron James is a better basketballer than Michael Jordan or where Steph Curry, Kevin Durant, and Kawhi Leonard rank. Dogs aren't often identified as caring about whether their beliefs about the Great Pumpkin are true or caring even whether they have any beliefs about the Great Pumpkin. And although dogs are much more likely than cats to care about seeing a beautiful sunset, that care—if it exists in dogs—is pretty small. And dogs certainly seem to care very little about hungry dogs in foreign lands, or even hungry dogs next door.

Furthermore, some would argue that humans, really, don't care about anything other than themselves. All that really matters to each of us is ourselves, you may believe. As an empirical claim, as a testable claim that you can support by observation, there is little to say in support of this claim.[6] We certainly seem to care about whether our beliefs are true or false, even when the beliefs in question have no apparent bearing upon our own lives and well-being. I suspect you care little about where I was born and that right now you hold no beliefs about that matter. But if you were to believe something about where I was born, you would prefer that belief to be true. Even if the belief doesn't really matter for you, has no apparent impact upon what you will eat for dinner tonight or any other part of your life, you would prefer it to be true, or at least not a silly or irrational thing to believe. As rational creatures, we humans just do care about our beliefs—not so much about holding lots of beliefs about lots of different things, but rather that whatever beliefs we do hold we hold for good reasons, or good enough reasons for the kinds of beliefs they are. And most of us care this way about most or all of our beliefs, and not only those of practical import.

This area of care—that is, caring that our beliefs are true, that we acquired these beliefs in the right sort of way (a more reliable way than just guessing or flipping a coin), that we hold them for good enough reasons, that we hold them about the right things and in the right way, with the right degree of tenacity or firmness—is called by philosophers the domain of *epistemology*. Epistemology is the philosophical examination of believing well and believing poorly, of excellences in believing and understanding, and of knowledge. Most philosophers believe, and most non-philosophers would agree, that we have duties when it comes to what and how we believe, that we have *epistemic obligations*. If you were to discover that I am an inveterate liar, you might be lost and confused when you hear me speak. Some of the things I say you already believe to be true; perhaps you know them to be true. But you also know that I am a liar and likely to be lying in at least some of what I say. You may be at a loss when it comes to much of what I say, but you would think you have a duty not to believe everything I say. Perhaps you should not believe me when I tell you what philosophers believe about duties. After all, as a rational being, you should not believe, at least not without

---

6. Psychologist C. Daniel Batson has conducted experiments that provide evidence against this claim. See his *Altruism in Humans*.

some sort of evidence or corroboration, what an inveterate liar tells you. You trust the testimony of some people, but not everyone, because you care about believing well.

We humans care about believing well and we care about not violating any of our duties of belief. We know that sometimes we are lost and confused in our beliefs, and we make efforts to try to find ourselves, to try to find what beliefs we should hold, all things being equal, about the issue at hand. Should I believe that much global climate change is anthropogenic? Could a rational person believe that rising sea levels are best explained by erosion, by massive stones and land falling into our oceans? What should I believe about the safety of consuming genetically modified crops? What does a rational person believe about how big the universe is or how long the universe will last? Am I violating any of my epistemic obligations in believing in God and in trusting God? We *care* whether our beliefs are true and whether we are violating any of our epistemic duties in believing what we believe.

In many cases our concerns are about believing the right things. In our earlier examples of being lost, that is, of not knowing one's place in a musical score during rehearsal, of being uncertain whether one may sell one's eggs or other body parts, of not knowing how the United States or any other nation should respond to terrorism or whether Christians may ever participate in war, and of lacking the satisfaction that we have lived our lives well, we want good, or right, beliefs. Concerns for holding true beliefs are *epistemic concerns*. But, in fact, given how many different things we believe and how many different things we could hold beliefs about, many of our examples above do seem to focus upon a certain area or domain of human life and human action. One significant component of living well, most of us believe, has to do with what we should or should not feel and do when it comes to other people. We might call this the *moral realm* or *morality*. Roughly speaking, the moral realm involves what we owe to one another and the concern that human beings are treated appropriately and that all persons are given the consideration that they deserve by virtue of their being human. The moral realm has to do with what is good for human beings and how we should act toward humans and, perhaps, other entities as well. But certainly, at least, humans. A good part of living well, it seems to most of us, is living morally.

Here, I think, although the epistemological realm overlaps with the moral realm, they are not identical. You and I do want to hold true beliefs about morality and how humans should regard and treat one another, because we value true beliefs and we recognize our epistemic obligations to believe well. We care about believing and believing well. Our concern with believing well, however, seems neither the only nor the primary reason we want to hold fitting and true moral beliefs. We want to hold true moral beliefs because we care about human life and humans living together and living well together. We care that other human beings (and not just we ourselves) are treated the way they deserve to be treated. We care about holding true beliefs about how we should treat others, and we care, too, that we act upon these true beliefs and in ways that comport well with these true beliefs about what we owe to others.

Much as we think we have epistemic obligations, most of us believe we also have *moral obligations.* We often find ourselves lost in knowing exactly what these moral obligations are and what they require us to do or be. Sometimes this is because of some particular circumstances of the other person, say someone who is very near to us or someone who is very far away, spatially or temporally. What do I owe people struggling to survive in Yemen? What do I owe my grandchildren? Sometimes we find ourselves lost in knowing what we owe to some particular type of human, say a seriously mentally impaired human, or a human in utero. Nevertheless, we think we do have moral obligations to other persons, whatever our uncertainty about the nature or content of those obligations. We want to hold the right moral beliefs because *we want to do what is good or what we think right,* and we believe that holding the right belief about what is good and right contributes to performing the good or right action, contributes to *our doing what is good or right.*

We care about living well with and toward other human beings. We care about other persons, and because we care about other persons, we care about living a moral life, about morality and our moral obligations to others. But although knowledge, that is, believing what we ought to believe and believing these things for the right sorts of reasons, and morality, or treating human beings and other valuable entities as they are worthy of being treated, are both important aspects of a good life, few of us think that these are the only things that matter for living well. Beauty, also, is a good thing. All things being equal, a life with significant experiences of beauty is one that is better than one with fewer or no significant experiences of beauty. All of us think pleasure is valuable. And achievements of some sort. And love, friendships, and family. And, perhaps, a relationship with God. Health, too, seems to be good. And, as we will later see, the list goes on. There are lots of good things and good types of experiences out there. So, our lives, if we are lucky, can go many different directions and can include a variety of good things. But which good things should matter the most to us? And how should these matter to us? May I choose to pursue beauty even if it means less attention to friends and family? This area of living well with respect to all the different goods and different types of goods is another area, overlapping with (or perhaps encompassing) the domains of knowledge and morality, in which we can find ourselves deeply lost.

It's important to remember here, too, that in our pursuit of a good life, very few, probably none, of us are solitary individuals making these decisions alone. Most of us not only must discover what should matter to us and how much these things should matter to us, we must consider others we are related to and their attempt to live well at the same time we are trying to live well. Our lives are intertwined. In *The Moon and Sixpence*, a novel loosely based upon the life of the artist Paul Gauguin, W. Somerset Maugham tells the story of Charles Strickland, a London stockbroker, who abandons his family and moves to Tahiti in pursuit of the good life, as an artist. But can we live well if we turn away from those nearest and dearest to us in order to live well? How do the claims of others upon us matter as we seek to live a good life? These are challenging questions, hard to find one's way around. It's easy to feel lost and hard not to realize that one's being lost may have serious consequences for others.

1.3 ON BEING MORALLY LOST AND TRYING TO FIND ONE'S WAY

So, in addition to there being an epistemic domain and epistemic values and duties, most of us believe there is a moral realm with its moral values and duties and that both of these are parts of living well as humans. This realm of the good life seems to be an area of choices and actions, choices to do and perhaps choices to feel, or at least try to have feelings about, one thing rather than another—for example, the choice to try feeling sympathy sometimes rather than schadenfreude[7]—choices to attempt to bring about or achieve some things rather than others. By and large, because this area is about life and living life, it includes lots of other parts of our lives, or the roles we play. I was born a son and a brother, and I can live well or poorly in these roles; I can be an angry son and a jealous brother or a grateful son and a kind brother. And being an angry son or a kind brother is not just one thing I do or feel, but a whole bunch of things. It is no wonder that, even though I have been in these roles as long as I can remember—as theologian Oliver O'Donovan has it, "we awake to our moral experience" and our moral roles

---

7. This German word refers to the joy or pleasure we feel in perceiving another person's misfortune.

just as we awake to our experience of the world[8]—sometimes I am confused, sometimes I don't know, what it means to be a good son or brother.

I am also a friend, an employee, a spouse, a citizen of my hometown, my state, and my country. I can be lost when it comes to knowing how to live well in each and every one of these areas, and I can be lost in lots of different ways about lots of different things, things that range from how much money I should spend on shoes to whether I should laugh at your jokes or feel sympathy for you when your girlfriend dumps you. I can also be lost and ignorant of what it looks like to live well when it comes to my life as a whole, when I'm not thinking about my responsibilities in any single part of my life but, instead, thinking about my whole life. We can wonder what a good human life looks like, a life that will undoubtedly include many of the roles mentioned above but that includes more than these specific roles. And even if there are many different ways of living well—and that's a question worth exploring—it does seem that we can identify at least some specific ways of life, some ways of inhabiting or performing various roles, that are *not* part of living well. But which are the better and the best ways for you or for me to live a worthy life?

Perhaps we more readily admit ignorance and confusion about specific roles we inhabit than about a well-lived life as a whole. After all, we may think we can secure expert advice about those roles and what a good way of performing those roles looks like. If I want to know how to be a good employee where I work, I can ask my boss or others in the business who seem to be doing well. If I want to know how to live well as a student, I can ask my teachers and the head of the school. If I want to live well as a son, I can ask my grandmothers and grandfathers. And so on.

Possibly, we don't think that way about living well as a human being; maybe we think there are no experts when it comes to living one's life well. Perhaps this is because we think there are no answers, no truths to discover about living life well. Or, perhaps, we simply assume we know where we are going and we follow whatever ways those around us are following. We stay on the dance floor as long as the music is playing. In other words, although this area of living our lives well is an area in which, upon reflection, we recognize that we can be lost, the experience of feeling lost, the awareness that one may in fact be lost, may be relatively rare, herd animals that we are. That we may be lost is a thought that may too infrequently cross our minds, especially in this place and at this time when our lives are so filled with noise and distractions.

---

8. O'Donovan, *Self, World, and Time*, 2.

So perhaps we can live well or we can live poorly with respect to lots of different things in many different areas or roles of life as well as in life as a whole. Sometimes our lives do not go well for us; accidents and illnesses strike us or those we love. And sometimes our lives do go well for us, though perhaps not because of anything we have chosen or done. The rain falls and the sun shines on the just and the unjust alike. And sometimes we live poor lives or good lives *because* of our choices, because of what we do or because of what we feel (though exactly how much of what we feel is a matter of what we have chosen is another question worth thinking about). If I choose to spend any extra money I have on soda pop and Little Debbies rather than on assisting those who are poor and genuinely hungry, mightn't I be living a poor life in multiple ways? Isn't a life in which one at least sometimes gives money to the genuinely needy a better life in some important ways than a life in which one never gives money to the genuinely needy, no matter how healthy and wealthy one is in every other aspect of her life?

If no one will hire me because of my criminal record, my life is not going well for me in some significant ways; I am not flourishing as a worker. But if I am kind to others, then, despite my life going poorly in some important ways, isn't my life well lived in other important ways? If I don't really care about the difficulties my elderly parents face, I am not living well as a son. If I care about their difficulties, even if I can do little or nothing to mitigate those difficulties, isn't it possible that I am living better than I otherwise would be? And so on. I can live well or I can live poorly in individual roles or areas of my life (and over a wide span of time), but I also want my life as a whole to be lived well. And this is true of all reflective persons.

Can we say anything more about this task of thinking and reasoning about living a good life, living the way we should live, about which questions and concerns are central and which are peripheral? I've talked about whether an action or a feeling is a good or bad or, perhaps, evil one, whether we ought or ought not to do or feel something, about whether something is right or wrong. This language of ought/should and good/bad implies standards or norms of some type, that is to say, something is good or right or something we ought to do or feel because it comports well with or fits, and does not violate, some relevant norm or standard. And something is bad or wrong or something we ought not to do because it does violate some relevant standard or norm. Why is it wrong, if indeed it is, to say or write, "Thank you for giving Casee and I the opportunity to speak to you," even if it is said by a vice president of something or other? Because it violates a rule of grammar (wherever that rule came from, a question for some other study).[9] But the norms we are talking about are much more significant than norms of grammar. If you ought to feel remorse after you kick me (and, lest there be any doubt, you should!), it's because there is some standard or norm of some sort that kicking someone like me violates and because there is another standard or norm of some sort that feeling remorse is an appropriate response to one's intentionally doing something that violates a norm such as this one.[10]

This helps a little, but only a little. First of all, there are norms and standards for all sorts of areas of our life that would seem to have little or nothing to do with living well or poorly in the way we are thinking about. However important it may be that you use "me" and "I" properly (and refrain from using "myself"), that you adhere to the current standards of good grammar, not many of us think your violation of those norms significantly impacts how well you live your life. (And we know those standards of grammar and word use change.) We may suspect that many of those who have lived worthy lives have paid little or no attention to the norms and standards of good grammar. Likewise, there are norms and standards for running a fast half-marathon, norms and standards for investing one's money, norms and standards for looking good, and norms and standards for providing attributions for some image you repost online, and so on.

The language of *norms* or *standards* can be misleading because it is ambiguous in other ways as well. Sometimes when we talk about norms we are talking about averages with respect to some behavior or feature of an individual or group. There is a norm for which hand is used dominantly—85 to 90 percent of humans are right-handed. There are social and cultural norms: where I live, the "done" thing is to call me "sir" and my wife "ma'am." There are norms in games: in chess, "Never give up your queen"; in baseball, "Don't bunt on a third strike." There are norms and standards of style and appearance: socks should match—except when they shouldn't. And so on. The point is that we appeal to "norms and standards" and we use the language of "good" and "bad," "right" and "wrong," "ought" and "ought not," in many different areas and in many different ways. You may think I ought not to have worn a plaid pink shirt with my plaid purple-and-yellow pants, but you are unlikely to think I have done some *moral* wrong in my choice of clothes. (This is not to say that one couldn't do moral wrong in

9. For those who are interested, the rule, roughly, is that "I" is a subject pronoun, a doer of something, and "me" is an object pronoun, a done-to something. The exception to the rule is "state-of-being" verbs, which you can pretty easily avoid using.

10. To be clear, I think the problem is performing a wrong or evil action of some sort. The problem is not violating the rule or standard that states that the wrong or evil action is morally impermissible.

one's choice of clothes.) Whether one's use of one's hand fits with the norm about right-handedness is not relevant, we think, to the matter of *morality* or to the matter of whether one is living well one's life as a whole.

1.4 FINDING ONE'S WAY

How to live well, how to live a good life, *who* to be and *how* to be the sort of person one ought to be is a very important thing—and, I've suggested, a very confusing thing for everybody. It is something almost all of us care about, and not only Christians, post-Christians, and those who are "spiritual but not religious," but also those who are neither spiritual nor religious. How do we find our way when it comes to living well?

A great medieval Jewish philosopher, Moses Maimonides (1135–1204), concerned with this question as well as many other philosophical problems, entitled his most important work *A Guide for the Perplexed*. I intend this small book as a guide for the perplexed—primarily for those who are perplexed about living a good life as a Christian and for those who *should be* perplexed about the Christian moral life. (I hope that in reading this first chapter some of those previously not perplexed have become at least a little perplexed.) Some of those who are perplexed may be Christian, but others will be those who want to understand what Christians do or should believe about living well even if they are more comfortable with the "spiritual but not religious" label or the "none" label. Living well, living a good life, should be a concern for everyone, whatever their self-understanding and worldview. The questions, the problems, are to a great extent the same, although we should not be surprised to find that the answers differ, as does the way of arriving at them. Understanding what living well looks like is an important goal and a goal we do well not to delay until late in our lives, as Ivan Ilych teaches us. It is an epistemically worthy goal and, I suspect and hope, a morally worthy goal, an important step toward living well.

There are many places we might start in trying to find a way through this subject. One good place to begin our journey is by trying better to understand something all persons have in common. What does it mean to be somebody, to be a self, to have an identity, a character? That is our topic for chapter 2.

The Road Ahead: A Prayer of Thomas Merton

My Lord God,

I have no idea where I am going. I do not see the road ahead of me. I cannot know for certain where it will end. Nor do I really know myself, and the fact that I think I am following your will does not mean that I am actually doing so. But I believe that the desire to please you does in fact please you. And I hope I have that desire in all that I am doing. I hope that I will never do anything apart from that desire. And I know that if I do this you will lead me by the right road, though I may know nothing about it. Therefore will I trust you always though I may seem to be lost and in the shadow of death. I will not fear, for you are ever with me, and you will never leave me to face my perils alone.[11]

Put Down the Phone: For Further Thought

1. Do you think we can ever really be lost when it comes to morality and living a good life? What explanation could we give for this being lost, if indeed we were? Why are we lost? How could we lose our way?

2. Is being lost always (and only) a matter of *knowing* or *not knowing* something? Or can one be lost, say, emotionally? What would be an example of this?

3. Could a person who is morally lost really know she is lost? Or would knowing you were lost indicate that you had at least to some extent found your way? Could a person who is morally lost prefer not to find her way?

4. Identify a time when you have been lost, morally speaking. What was the issue of the situation? Were you able somehow at last to find your way? How?

5. All this talk about being "morally lost" suggests that one could be morally "found" and know that one knows where one is, morally speaking. How would you go about persuading someone that you know where you are with respect to some moral issue, for example, whether one should cheat on one's spouse? Could only another "morally not lost" person understand and be persuaded by your argument? Why or why not?

6. If morality is fundamentally about values, about what we do value and what we should value (and how much we should value the various things we do value), where do these values come from?

---

11. Merton, *Thoughts in Solitude*, 79.

7. Why does it make sense to think of Dietrich Bonhoeffer as lost? About what things do you think he was lost? Are there things he would say he was sure about, and not lost? What would these be?

8. In addition to moral values, what other types of values can you identify?

2

BRAND, IDENTITY, AND BEING SOMEBODY
(and Knowing Who You Are)

2.1 WHAT'S YOUR BRAND?

It doesn't take long for things to trickle down from the world of business and permeate the personal realm. In the last half a dozen or so years, one business practice that has become increasingly prominent for individuals is *branding*. Businesses present themselves to consumers in certain ways so that when we hear their names we think things like *reliable, creative, cool, strong*, or *trustworthy*. It can work the same way in our personal lives, and we are encouraged to learn from business practices and to think about how we want to present ourselves to others in our world of social media. What's your brand? What perceptions do you want others to have of you? How should you present yourself in order to have others think of you in the ways you want?

If you are uncertain about your brand, not to worry: there are plenty of online quizzes to assist you in discovering your brand archetype. (I'm a maven. Or maybe a caregiver/hero/innocent. It's complicated, I guess.) We do care about how people perceive us, and the pressure to present ourselves well to others has greatly intensified in recent years as the avenues for presenting ourselves have increased. Instagram, Twitter, Snapchat—and even Facebook for folks like me.

But branding is the world of perception, the world of appearance, not reality. At the end of the day, you and I want to put down our phones, because we want to just *be* and to stop presenting ourselves for others. But who are we? Who are you, really? Is your personal brand what it should be, in light of who you really are? Or is it just how you prefer that people think of you? Is there a real you or, instead, a bunch of yous, slipping in and sliding away as you go through your life? How easy is it to say who you are, really, at least right now?

We often think that one of the great things about moving to a new place—a new school, a new city, a new country—is that we can't get lost because there is no there there, no person or place that we have to be. Nobody knows us, so nobody has much in the way of clear expectations of us. We can be anybody we choose to be, wherever we want to be. We can re-create ourselves with completely new identities, we may think. We can't be lost, at least when it comes to knowing who we are, because we can create new identities, be a new person, even a number of different persons, should we choose.

But that feeling rarely lasts. We do things, and then we regret having done them. We decide that ouzo, or clubbing all night, or taking a selfie with every good-looking person we see, or asking people to call us "Spyros" or "Claudette" doesn't work for us after all. That is not who we really are, and people who know us in those ways don't really know us.

2.2 WHO ARE YOU?

What would it mean for someone to know you, to *really* know you? If there are people who know you, what do they know about you? They probably know what their senses tell them about you: how you look, that is, what your body looks like, your size or skin color, how you stand and how you sit, how you smell, how you sound when you speak and when you breathe, and maybe how salty your skin tastes. We can learn a lot about others by paying attention to them, by close observation of what is perceivable. But you and I also think that a person could know all those things people perceive about us and still not really know *us*, that we are deeper and possibly different than what can be known about us by the senses. Perhaps you might say that a person could know your body and still not know the real you, that you are more than your body. Maybe you would call this "more" your soul or your true or best self.[1]

What is this more that is you? What is the real you, in addition to your body?[2] What are some of the bits of the real you that others cannot perceive directly? What, other than our bodies, makes you you and makes me me? We can start with our *wants* or *desires*; we are desiring things. Many of our desires are similar to the wants or desires of others, many of them are different. From infancy, from our earliest hours, you and I want many things and we perform actions to get them. We want food, so we cry and fidget. We want sleep, so we cry and we fidget. We want a tender caress and cooing sounds, so we, yes, cry and fidget. As we grow, the range of our desires expands. We desire silence, we desire something yellow, we desire a good story, we want that big furry four-legged thing not to come too close to us. As we mature, we can, as Alasdair MacIntyre points out, come to understand our desires and we begin to distinguish one from another by the *objects* of our desires, by *what* we want.[3] I don't want a bath, I want to eat a hot Krispy Kreme donut. You want a fifteen-minute nap. He just wants to bang on the drum all day. You and I, unlike infants, usually know the object of our desire. We have *beliefs*, some of which are about what we desire. I believe a pat on the back will make me feel better about things, so I would like someone to pat me on my back. I believe a hot Krispy Kreme donut will taste good right now; that belief explains my desire for the donut.[4] I want you to be on my basketball team because I believe you play good defense (though you need

---

1. An important question arises here. If a person can know your body without really knowing you, without knowing your soul or your true self, could a person know the real you, that is, your soul or your self, without also knowing your body? Plato (and those who follow him) certainly seemed to think so, at least in principle. Plato thought of the body as a kind of prison for our souls, our real selves, and writes of Socrates describing philosophy as preparation or "training for death," the release of the soul from its bodily prison. (See Plato's *Phaedo*, 61c–69e.) Plato maintains that our selves, our true identities, bear no necessary connection to our bodies. Our bodies are temporary containers for our immaterial, eternal souls. Christians, in practice, may hold rather Platonic views. But in affirming in the creeds "the resurrection of the body and the life everlasting," rather than, say, the disappearance of the body but the resurrection of the soul, Christians are much more "worldly" than Plato and, perhaps, much more paradoxical (or, worse yet, contradictory).

2. We should note that transgender persons may believe that the body they inhabit is, at times, not really them—that there is a disconnect between themselves, who they really are, and their bodies for at least some of their lives.

3. MacIntyre, *Ethics in the Conflicts of Modernity*, 2.

4. Or, perhaps, that desire explains my belief; we need not now commit ourselves to a particular view of the direction or directions that the belief-desire relation runs.

to stop shooting so many threes). We believe there are few things sweeter than a young child's laugh, so we want to hear children at play.

Our beliefs seem often to inform and guide our desires. Unlike infants, in adults the *desire* and the *felt need* are not identical. The infant feels hungry and desires to eat. The baby feels gaseous and wants to be held. In contrast, adults can recognize and feel a need that they may not want to satisfy (or that they may want *not* to satisfy), at least not at this or that particular time. I can feel hungry yet not desire to eat at this moment because I am getting ready to go for a run.

We also have wants or desires about our wants and desires, that is to say, we have "second-order desires" about our "first-order desires," the things we want. Sometimes we want to want what we want; not only do I want to spend time practicing piano tonight, I want to want that, for I believe that wanting to practice piano will lead to my playing better and I also want to play better. And sometimes we wish not to satisfy some desire, perhaps because satisfaction of that desire will interfere with some future we want. You really want to punch me in the nose but you also really wish you didn't want to punch me, for punching me will result in your expulsion from school and you want to stay in school, so you count to ten and walk away. Or, I can want a sixth hot Krispy Kreme donut, but because I believe that if I have a sixth donut I will need to add two more miles to my eight-mile run tomorrow, I can also want not to want what I want. You can want to stay in bed rather than go to class, but stay in bed and you fail the test, and fail the test and there goes grad school. And you can want not to be tempted to lie or cheat as frequently as you seem to be tempted.

Also, as MacIntyre points out, adults are aware not only of their future desires, but also of their past desires.[5] Adults are aware of the history of their desires, and our understanding of both what our desires have been in the past and how they may move us toward or distract us from a future we want for ourselves shapes our second-order desires about our first order-desires. We know that we are not slaves to any of our current desires, for we are aware that we have abandoned, exchanged, and lost many of our earlier wants and desires and have created and discovered new wants and desires.

Desires, whether they are transitory or more permanent, are but part of what makes us who we are, makes you or me some particular self. We are what we want and what we want to want, but that is not all we are. In addition to desires, we have feelings and we have *emotions*. My arm hurts and I am sad that you broke my arm when you blocked my shot. You are anxious about the grade you will get on your paper. We also have likes and dislikes,

5. MacIntyre, *Ethics in the Conflicts of Modernity*, 3.

that is to say, *affections* and their objects. You like the colors blue and orange. You dislike riding in the car when your father is driving. You hate how your brother is always "mansplaining" things. And as we've seen, we have *beliefs*, like our affections and emotions, informing and shaping what we want and how we act upon our wants, and being informed and shaped by other beliefs, desires, affections, and emotions. My aunt believes that for every drop of rain that falls a flower grows, so she lives hopefully. I believe it will be hot and muggy again tomorrow and I want to be cool and to look cool, so I plan to wear my favorite short-sleeved shirt. (And, as a student recently told me, I should believe that I have a right to "bare arms.") We have *tastes*. I prefer running in dark-colored shorts and bright orange Dri-fit tees. You dig Coltrane, but you've never really cared for Ornette Coleman. Or Kenny G. Best not to get you started on Kenny G.

Add to our desires, emotions, tastes, affections, and beliefs our *habits*. These are stable dispositions of conduct, or tendencies to act and/or dispositions to feel certain ways under certain conditions. I tend to adjust my hair by running my left hand through it. If cookies are offered, I tend to choose oatmeal-raisin rather than chocolate chip. You don't litter; you do recycle, although not frequently, because you very rarely use single-use plastics or glass. You do not laugh at jokes that belittle others. You usually use a blue pen for signing your name and you hold the pen with your index and middle fingers atop the pen.

We also have *cares* about things, belief-attitude-desire combinations expressed in *commitments* that guide our actions. Some things matter to us, others don't matter or don't matter so much. You care that your sister is not lonely, so you want to visit her. You care about whether your garden and yard are pretty, so you tend them. You care about making beautiful music, so you practice your cello. Cares can be trivial (and we can know them to be trivial) or they can be of the greatest import to us. I may care deeply about whether I can consistently nail three-point shots, and I may organize my days to get more practice in on my threes, while at the same time I may recognize that this is not at all genuinely important for someone at my age and stage of life. Our cares and commitments guide and direct what we feel, what we see, and what we do in significant as well as relatively insignificant ways. Cares orient us to what is important or valuable for our lives and underwrite our intuitions about what is good and what makes our lives meaningful.

All these things together—our desires, emotions, tastes, habits, beliefs, cares, and commitments, however we acquired them, however they came to be ours—make up our characters. They make us the selves we are. So we are likely to think that someone who knows us knows more than how we appear; they know our character, they know our deep selves, they know the constellation of desires, emotions, tastes, habits, beliefs, cares, and commitments that we are. We are, to be sure, our bodies. We are also our desires, and "emotions, tastes, affections, habits, and beliefs"[6]—and cares and commitments.

Each of these areas has its own object or "aboutness." If you are feeling fearful, you are fearful of something.[7] Enjoyment is always the enjoyment of something, say, walking in a forest on a moonlit night. And so on. You desire a personal record (a "PR") in your next half-marathon. I love my children. You enjoy, you dig, listening to the album *Bill Evans at the Montreux Jazz Festival*. We like to chat with one another over coffee. Daily, you say a prayer when you rise in the morning and when you go to bed in the evening. I believe that God will not forsake us. You may believe that the arc of the moral universe is long and that it bends toward justice. We don't just *care*, period. My caring has an object—my son's flourishing, my health, clean rivers, and so on.[8]

Among our many, many beliefs, as we saw in our first chapter, are beliefs about beliefs, about believing rightly, beliefs about our epistemic obligations, that is, about believing what we ought to believe and not violating any epistemic duties of believing. Because we are rational, we care about whether we are believing what we should, about whether we are acting as rational creatures in our believing. Should I believe that there are terrorists from the Middle East on the migrant caravan simply because it is possible that there are and because we don't know definitively that they aren't there? But if that were epistemically required of us, then wouldn't we also have an obligation to believe that there are terrorists in the White House since that, too, is logically possible and we don't know definitively that there are no terrorists in the White House? Is that reasonable? Do we violate our epistemic obligations when we believe things about which we are not certain? That would be a very high bar for permissible beliefs, for there are very few propositions about which we can be certain. As I've learned from Descartes, I can be certain that I exist whenever I am thinking about my existence.[9] But how much more can I be certain of?

6. MacIntyre, *Ethics in the Conflicts of Modernity*, 3.

7. Moods, unlike emotions, appear to lack a specific object. If you are gloomy, there is no particular thing about which you are gloomy. Everything has a gloomy cast.

8. I leave it to the reader to determine whether First Lady Melania Trump's "I really don't care . . ." is a counterexample to the claim that our cares have objects or "aboutnesses." See https://www.cnn.com/2018/06/21/politics/melania-trump-jacket/index.html.

9. See Descartes, *Meditations on First Philosophy*.

We also have seen that almost all of us have beliefs about what is permissible and what is impermissible in how we treat other people. We are *social* beings; we care about living together. So, we have beliefs about *morality*, about what we owe to others, about our moral obligations, our duties not to harm others (duties of non-malevolence) as well as our duties to help others (duties of beneficence). Much as we have desires and beliefs about fulfilling our epistemic obligations, we have beliefs and desires about what we owe to others and about not violating our moral obligations. We feel remorse or we feel guilty when we violate our moral duty not to harm others. We want to do better in how we treat strangers in our community. We feel a special respect and admiration for those who are adept at recognizing and fulfilling their moral obligations.

And we have epistemic habits as well as moral habits. Habits, too, like desires, affections, emotions, and beliefs, have their objects or "aboutnesses." As we'll see later, we can think of *virtues* as habits of a special type, as human excellences, as dispositions to feel or act we should seek to possess because they make us better at being the sorts of creatures we should be and doing things we should be doing. There are different types of virtues—*intellectual virtues*, for example, those habits that enable us to believe well and to satisfy our epistemic obligations. And *practical virtues*, habits of practice, of acting toward other people and objects. Some of these are habits or dispositions that dispose us to behave well toward other people and objects of moral value, to give others what is due to them and not to violate moral obligations. Moral virtues are *moral traits of character*, fixed or stable tendencies to feel and act in certain ways under certain conditions. Some of these are habits or dispositions that dispose us to behave appropriately toward or in the presence of certain objects presented to us for our consideration, or what we might call *aesthetic traits of character*. No doubt, there are other types of virtues as well.

Let's consider the moral virtue of kindness. A kind person is a person who habitually benefits others in fitting and welcome ways. A kind person can't help noticing (whether or not she is aware that she is noticing) when a smile or a good word would benefit another, so she smiles or says a good word. A kind person has a knack for the right word or the right look at the right time for you, knows and does what will lift you up when you are down. As MacIntyre puts it, virtues are habits or "dispositions to act and to react in . . . patterned ways,"[10] fixed dispositions to have the right feelings "at the right times, about the right things, toward the right people, for the right

10. MacIntyre, *Ethics and the Conflicts of Modernity*, 7.

end, and in the right way" and to act in a way that comports well with these feelings, as Aristotle argues.[11]

To be somebody, to have a character, then, is to possess a body of particular desires, preferences, and tastes; emotions and affections; beliefs, some of these having as their objects what and how we should believe and what and how we should act; and habits. Some of these habits are intellectual and practical habits, that is, intellectual and practical virtues, and some, but not all, of them moral virtues.

2.3 WHAT'S LOVE GOT TO DO WITH IT?

To put things just this way is misleading, for it leaves out our *cares*. It is hard to speak very clearly and precisely about this area of "cares" and all that it may include, but it is no less crucial for an understanding of character and who we are and for making sense of ourselves for that. We have cares not only about what is right, not only about believing rightly and acting rightly, doing what we ought to do when it comes to believing and doing. We do have cares about what is right and what is true, but we also have cares about what is good and what is beautiful, about what is admirable and what we enjoy immensely. We have beliefs and attitudes about what is choice-worthy, about what one should desire, about what one should love, about what one should feel and how one should act, and some sense of how things are going in our life. Our cares are arranged and prioritized, as philosopher Charles Taylor puts it, in "an orientation to the good,"[12] a direction in life toward which we aim and in light of which we assess how well things are going for us.

To better grasp *cares*, so central to our identities and to how we live our lives and understand ourselves, and to see how cares are distinct from the other areas we've discussed, we might consider love and its role in our lives. When it comes to our epistemic duties, when it comes to believing rightly, we can pretty much say what needs to be said without making any reference to what we love. I satisfy my obligation to believe well when I act as a rational agent, proportioning the tenacity of my belief to the grounds or evidence of the belief that are currently available to me. For example, if I believe that it is likely to rain tomorrow because you have told me so, but I also believe you have only about 60 percent accuracy in your weather predictions, I won't firmly hold my belief that it will rain. So if Mike, whom I regard as a great authority on the weather, tells me I can leave my umbrella

11. Aristotle, *Nicomachean Ethics*, 1106b.

12. Taylor, *Sources of the Self*, 33–34.

at home tomorrow, I will let go of my belief that it will rain. The firmness with which I hold on to a belief should track the reliability of the means by which I have acquired the belief. Love needn't enter the picture when it comes to satisfying our epistemic obligations.

The same seems true of our moral duties as I have characterized them. I satisfy my obligation to behave well toward others when I violate no moral duties I have to others, when I do no harm to others and when I benefit them in at least some minimal way. I can do these things, fulfill these obligations, without loving the recipients of my actions. I can respect my duty not to harm others and even to promote their well-being without loving them. Apparently, love needn't enter the picture.

But consider how little these two realms of duty—epistemic and moral—appear to overlap with our cares, with what is most important to us, with our loves and our values, with the things that we think make our lives meaningful. If my child is crying and I ask myself only, "What are the duties and obligations I have to this child?" hasn't something gone dreadfully wrong? Instead, shouldn't my care for, my love for, my commitment to my child be my first thought? Isn't love what guides the good parent? Isn't being a good parent, or a good brother or sister or son or daughter, about caring for others, about loving others?

The objects of our loves are many and varied. Persons are among the objects of our love, but not only other persons but also animals, ideas, activities like reading or playing piano, foods, understanding and other achievements, beauty, justice, God, contentment, and flourishing. We love, we care for, many, many things, large and small. Some of these loves may have to do with morality, with moral duties, but most do not. Because we care for and about these many things, big and small, we identify ends or goals by which we direct our actions. We orient ourselves to that which we love.

Our loves, and likewise our beliefs and attitudes, habits, emotions and affections, desires, preferences, and tastes, need not be permanent (though to the extent that they are our characters are more or less stable). Each of these may characterize us to varying degrees, and we may hold to them with more or less firmness and tenacity. You may be invited out for dinner and discover cilantro, and that may revolutionize your taste in food and lead you to abandon your habit of always ordering a cheeseburger when you go out to eat. Your new goal is to expand your familiarity with the many and varied uses of cilantro in cooking. Or you may come to realize that that boy band you used to think was so great was, in reality, just another boy band and you may now care more about listening to Django Reinhardt. (And well you should!)

These facets of our character are sometimes simple (e.g., I want a glass of water) and sometimes complex, consisting of a complicated web of desires, emotions, affections, tastes, habits, cares, and beliefs extending over time, extending into the future. *Projects* are complex desires for something not immediately available to us, for something that we might aim to receive or achieve at some point in the future. We care about real projects; we are committed to them. We think what we aim for, what we desire, that at which we aim, to be good and worthy of our pursuit. Its achievement matters to us. I may have a project of becoming an excellent cellist, or becoming a good spouse and parent. Some projects matter a great deal to us, while others we may embrace quite loosely. I may want to write a great novel, or I may want simply to learn how to cook kohlrabi so that it tastes good, and this only until rutabagas are more readily accessible to me; once the rutabagas are available, I will ignore kohlrabi.

Which projects should we embrace and pursue? Is the project of learning how to cook kohlrabi really worthy of my time and effort? And how should I prioritize those projects I embrace? Which should I care most about? Why? For what vocation should I prepare, given my loves and my projects? How much must I live for God or for my neighbor, given who I understand myself to be? If I give myself appropriately to the achievement of beauty or aesthetic excellence, or to any other achievement, must that be constrained by my love for and commitment to other goods of my life? How?

The answers to these and similar questions will come from how we orient ourselves to the good, will come from our cares and commitments, from our loves. From whom we understand ourselves to be. That understanding of ourselves, of who we are and who we will to be, is itself both gift and goal.

2.4 WE ARE NOT ALONE

In the normal course of our lives we acquire or develop cares and projects in much the same way that we acquire other desires, simple and complex. Perhaps I find myself desiring roasted tomatoes tonight because last Thursday you cooked dinner for me and served me a dish with roasted tomatoes (and olives and garlic!) that I enjoyed immensely, and just now, for some reason I can't identify, I noticed myself thinking about and wanting some roasted tomatoes. I want to learn to roast tomatoes and to cook with roasted tomatoes. So it is for many of our projects. You had no idea how good a mandolin could sound until your roommate played that track of Chris Thile playing a Bach sonata, and now you want to play the mandolin; now, you have a project of playing a Bach sonata on a mandolin.

This suggests the extent to which you and I are not completely authors of our own characters. We are never individuals whose identities exist independently of the community or communities in which we have been born and raised and currently live. The range of desires, projects, tastes, emotions, habits, beliefs, and cares available to us is both expanded as well as narrowed by the people with whom we have a history, for each of us is formed by others and always stands in some relation to a community in which we find ourselves. The philosopher F. H. Bradley summarized our interconnectedness with others from our very earliest days this way:

> Thus the child is . . . born not into a desert, but into a living world, a whole which has a true individuality of its own . . . [H]e has in him inherited habits, or what will of themselves appear as such; but, in addition to this, he is not for one moment left alone, but continually tampered with. . . . And yet the tender care that receives and guides him is impressing on him habits, habits, alas, not particular to himself, and the "icy chains" of universal custom are hardening themselves round his cradled life. As the poet tells us, he has not yet thought of himself; his earliest notions come mixed to him of things and persons, not distinct from one another, nor divided from the feeling of his own existence. The need that he cannot understand moves him to foolish, but not futile, cries for what only another can give him; and the breast of his mother, and the soft warmth and touches and tones of his nurse, are made one with the feeling of his own pleasure and pain; nor is he yet a moralist to beware of such illusion, and to see in them mere means to an end without them in his separate self. For he does not even think of his separate self; he grows with his world, his mind fills and orders itself; and when he can separate himself from that world, and know himself apart from it, then by that time his self, the object of his self-consciousness, is penetrated, infected, characterized by the existence of others. Its content implies in every fiber relations of community. He learns, or already perhaps has learned, to speak, and here he appropriates the common heritage of his race; the tongue that he makes his own is his country's language, it is (or it should be) the same that others speak, and it carries into his mind the ideas and sentiments of the race . . . and stamps them in indelibly. He grows up in an atmosphere of example and general custom, his life widens out from one little world to

other and higher worlds, and he apprehends through successive
stations the whole in which he lives, and in which he has lived.[13]

My self, my character, and the desires, tastes, emotions, affections, habits,
cares, and even beliefs that make me who I am, are formed, sometimes
consciously, often unconsciously, in community with others. I am neither
master of my soul nor captain of my fate, for I am not self-created. I am
formed in community with others. Each of us, as Charles Taylor argues,
exists within "webs of interlocution," in tangled conversations, in arguments
and agreements with some "defining community."[14]

This is not to claim that we are not authors or, perhaps better, coau-
thors of our characters. Our desires, tastes, and affections, as well as our
projects, may be developed and formed in interaction with others, but they
are not outside our control, or at least not completely outside our control.
We decide not to satisfy some desires, and as a result of that decision and the
behavior that expresses that decision, the desire is weakened, and perhaps
diminished to an almost unnoticeable register. We develop new projects for
ourselves. You may have had no interest in the accordion until I showed you
a video of Sharon Shannon and Steve Earle playing "Galway Girl," and now
you have a project of becoming a player of traditional Irish music on the
accordion (or at least a concertina). And the same is likely true of our beliefs
and cares. They may happen to us; we may find we have them but we are
not sure how we acquired them. Still, these beliefs or cares having happened
to us, we may yet have it in our power to alter them. We can work to care
more about some things and less about others. We may be able to position
ourselves to see the world differently, to come to believe that the world is not
as cruel and unkind as we had believed.

2.5 CHARACTER AND GROUND PROJECTS

Our identities, our characters, are complex. We are bundles or bunches or
webs of desires, tastes, affections, emotions, habits, beliefs, and cares, more
or less integrated and unified. Some of these are chosen or affirmed by our
community-shaped selves, others are "gifts" we may not even be aware of
having received. We are not, however, just a bunch of conflicting desires and
projects, driven by whichever desire or project is at some particular time
dominant. Just as we subordinate some desires to other desires or projects,
so we subordinate certain projects to other projects or desires. We typically

13. Bradley, *Ethical Studies*, 171–72.
14. Taylor, *Sources of the Self*, 36.

rank or prioritize our projects, our complex goals, sometimes privileging the achievement of speaking a second language fluently over playing first seat cello in the orchestra.

To have a relatively stable character, then, is to have one's desires and projects arranged in a pattern or identifiable constellation, that is to say, with some desires and projects regularly taking priority over others in our lives and with little or infrequent conflict between our various projects. As philosopher Bernard Williams noted, typically some projects are of markedly greater importance to an individual than are others. These "ground projects," as Williams calls them,[15] express our own orientation to the good and, perhaps, our orientation to the true and the beautiful as well. They express our loves, our values, what matters to us, what we care about, what we think worthy of our love or respect.

Our ground projects show what we think a good life and living well consists of; they direct our desires and our decisions about what we ought to do and what we ought not to do. But we should not assume that all our ground projects are related to living morally. For many of us, indeed, for most of us, to live well, to live a good life, is to aim to live at least a minimally moral life. Morality does matter to us, but morality, and being morally good, is not the only thing that matters to us. We care about our children, and that can sometimes pull us to caring and acting in ways that may violate moral standards of impartiality and so may not be morally good. We care about truth. We care about beauty. Some of us care, and care profoundly, about friendship, in particular friendship with God.

We may have a number of ground projects, and occasionally we may find ourselves with apparently competing or even conflicting ground projects. My ground project related to beauty may pull me in directions that drive me away from my ground project of being a morally good person. We'll need to leave it for later to determine what to do in such cases of conflict between one ground project and another. Suffice it to say that a concern for and commitment to living well, to living a good life, does not entail that the ground projects of morality should *always* take priority and trump all other ground projects, though many philosophers, Immanuel Kant chief among them, have thought so.

Ground projects are so fundamental to our self-understanding and our values that without these projects our lives would mean less to us. These are projects that ground us and upon which we build and organize our other projects and desires. You want to become fluent in Spanish, but although that is a project to which you are committed, it isn't a ground project for

15. Williams, "Persons, Character and Morality," 12–13.

you. You can very well imagine your life going on much the same as it is now going even if you never reach that goal. It isn't nearly as important to you as your project of loving God well, or your project of being a good neighbor or a good parent. Ground projects, Williams suggests, give meaning to one's life. They "propel us into the future"[16] by providing a powerful motivating force. They give us reason for living. As philosopher Susan Wolf says, "Meaning in life consists in and arises from actively engaging in projects of worth," that is to say, not only projects that we find worthy but projects that are in fact worthy, that we would be mistaken not to find worthy.[17]

Philosopher-theologian James K. A. Smith has written that we are what we love.[18] Our identities, who we are, are expressed most deeply and clearly in what we love. Our ground projects, the goals and goods of greatest value to us and those to which we are thoroughly committed, are what we love, are who we are. We are what we love; we are our ground projects, what we understand and pursue as essential for our living well, as giving meaning to our lives.

2.6. NARRATIVE, VIRTUES, AND CHARACTER

Charles Taylor has noted the difficulty most of us have in making sense of ourselves. In addition to understanding ourselves in relation to a defining community from whom we have learned to communicate about our world, and in addition to an orientation to what we believe and love as good, to understand ourselves we must think of our lives in terms of a *narrative*. We are storied creatures. Taylor writes,

> Thus making sense of my present action, when we are not dealing with such trivial questions as where shall I go in the next five minutes but with the issue of my place relative to the good, requires a narrative understanding of my life, a sense of what I have become which can only be given in a story. And as I project my life forward and endorse the existing direction or give it a new one, I project a future story, not just a state of the momentary future but a bent for my whole life to come.[19]

To understand ourselves, Taylor argues, we must have a story; we must be able to tell a story of ourselves, a story with a beginning, a middle, and an

---

16. Williams, "Persons, Character and Morality," 13.
17. Wolf, *Meaning in Life*, 26.
18. Smith, *You Are What You Love*.
19. Taylor, *Sources of the Self*, 48.

end at which we are aiming. Stories hang together; they are not merely a collection of events temporally arranged, not just one thing after another. Our stories must cohere and go somewhere if they are to help us understand ourselves.

And, again, you and I are not alone in trying to tell our stories. My narrative and your narrative intersect with the narratives of others, with none of us the sole authors of our stories. Alasdair MacIntyre makes this point clearly:

> Only in fantasy do we live what story we please. In life . . . we are always under certain constraints. We enter upon a stage which we did not design and we find ourselves part of an action that was not of our making. Each of us being a main character in his own drama plays subordinate parts in the dramas of others, and each drama constrains the others. In my drama, perhaps I am Hamlet or Iago or at least the swineherd who may yet become a prince, but to you I am only A Gentleman or at best Second Murderer, while you are my Polonius or my Gravedigger, but your own hero.[20]

What follows if we think of our lives as "narrative quests," to use MacIntyre's language, if we think of our lives as pursuits, as attempts to understand and to attain what we regard as good, as true, and as beautiful? It doesn't follow that we do not need to attempt to discern whether some actions are, of their nature, right or good, or whether we should always aim, by contrast, to achieve certain desirable outcomes. Determining what we ought to do and aiming in our actions at what is right and what is good is crucial for us as moral agents. But that is not the whole of the moral life, and the moral life is not the whole of our lives. The recognition of our duties and these acts we perform because they are right or good or beautiful will be intelligible and will make sense only if we see them as the acts of an agent with a certain character, agents who care wisely and well and who embody virtues in their actions and in their emotions, in what they feel and do.

Perhaps we might think of ourselves, whoever we are, as musicians. In this case, the story we wish to tell of ourselves is a story of performers of sweet music (if we are Christians, music sweet to the ears of God and to the ears of other living things as well as ourselves; others may recognize a different kind of sweetness). If that image of ourselves as musicians, as performers of a good life, captures how we should understand living our lives well, then we will need to draw upon a variety of types of information in learning to perform our lives well. We will need to learn what we should

20. MacIntyre, *After Virtue*, 213–14.

and should not do in our practice and our performance of the music; we will need to learn about the character of musicians and what traits great musicians possess. We will need to learn about music, and the music we are to perform. We will need to learn, as well, about the conductor.

And this is to say that fittingly orienting ourselves to God and the good and the place of morality and values in the performance of our lives in a fitting orientation to God and the good is no simple thing. In our world full of wonders and riches and distractions, of genuine goods and only apparent goods, it is easy, as we have seen, to lose one's way, to find oneself lost.

But this is to get far ahead of ourselves. Why should anyone, and why might Christians, in particular, think of their lives as a performance? Why might a Christian's orientation to the good, as well as others' orientations to the good, involve, or even require, understanding one's life as a performance? To answer this question, we will need to think more carefully about Christian identity, our project in chapter 3. But first, we might orient our thoughts with the assistance of a great twentieth-century American thinker, H. Richard Niebuhr.

Helmut Richard Niebuhr (1894–1962)

Like his older brother, Reinhold, the midwesterner H. Richard Niebuhr graduated from Elmhurst College in Illinois and Eden Theological Seminary near St. Louis before completing his studies at Yale Divinity School and Yale University, receiving his PhD in religion in 1924. Although like his brother he was ordained a pastor, his experience, unlike Reinhold's, was primarily academic. He taught first at Eden, his alma mater, and then returned to Elmhurst, where he served as president for three years. In 1931 he ventured back to Yale Divinity School, where he taught Christian ethics for three decades, until his death in 1962.

Richard was a complex thinker with interests in history and sociology as well as theology and philosophy. Although he was sympathetic to the concerns of the social gospel movement and its campaign for justice and equality, he considered the social gospel theology all too frequently on offer from the movement to be bland—and bland, perhaps, in an especially American way. In his *The Kingdom of God in America* (1937), Niebuhr characterized the theology of the social gospel this way: "A God without wrath brought men without sin into a kingdom without judgment through the ministrations of a Christ without a cross."[21]

---

21. Niebuhr, *Kingdom of God in America*, 193.

Niebuhr's most influential work, *Christ and Culture* (1951), examined Christian individuals and groups throughout the history of the faith, both how they understood God and the work of God in our world and how they understood themselves as called to respond to the work of God in the world. His most sophisticated work in moral thought appears in *The Responsible Self: An Exercise in Christian Moral Philosophy*, a work still incomplete at the time of his death. Published posthumously in 1963, this material available to us is based upon a series of lectures Niebuhr had presented.

Niebuhr's project in *The Responsible Self* is to examine and explain the human moral life as Christians understand it. He describes his work as a work in Christian moral philosophy rather than moral theology because his approach is "Bible-informed" but not "Bible-centered." He is quick to add a criticism of moral philosophy. Too frequently, the approach of moral philosophers is to treat the moral life as though it is non-historical, "as though the ideas and words of the English moral language referred to the pure emotions of non-historical beings or to pure concepts."[22] His is a work in Christian moral philosophy because he accepts the "fateful fact" of his having been born into a Christian family and because he identifies himself with what he understands to be "the cause of Jesus Christ," the reconciliation of all persons to God.[23] His ground projects include living as a follower of Jesus and attempting to understand and articulate how Christians might better live responsive to God's activity in the world.

Niebuhr proposes the concept of "responsibility" as fundamental for a true understanding of ourselves as moral agents. We are responders, acting in response to what we perceive to be going on in the world, with our interpretations of the acts of God as well as the acts of other persons. As Niebuhr puts it, "We attempt to answer the question: 'What shall I do?' by raising as the prior question: 'What is going on?' . . ."[24] To be responsible is to recognize that we are accountable to others; we are members of a "continuing community of agents" who have expectations of us, who have some claim upon us.[25] We are not alone. We cannot escape the gifts of others to us or the just demands of others upon us.

22. Niebuhr, *Responsible Self*, 46.
23. Niebuhr, *Responsible Self*, 43.
24. Niebuhr, *Responsible Self*, 63.
25. Niebuhr, *Responsible Self*, 65.

In developing his understanding of responsibility, Niebuhr distinguishes the responsible/responsive self from two alternative understandings or models of human morality. The person as maker understands the human moral role as primarily that of crafter and shaper and former and molder of reality in light of one's goals, as aiming to bring about some desirable outcomes, some aimed-for state of affairs. The person as maker understands herself primarily as moral agent aiming at the realization of the good. The person as citizen model highlights the right; our obedience to what is right must constrain the outcomes at which we aim. Our pursuit of goodness must be bound by our recognition of moral duties that protect who and what is valuable.

Niebuhr finds that neither of these two models adequately captures the breadth and depth of our experiences as moral agents. Although the purposeful life endorsed by the person as maker model and the obedient life of the person as citizen model capture important moral themes, these models cannot easily accommodate powerful, universal human experiences in which our understanding of ourselves as agents and our purposiveness are undercut. Consider human suffering and how illness may wreak havoc with one's actions and the goals one is seeking to achieve. "I might have been a . . . but for this sickness." Likewise, Niebuhr suggests that not only are the person as maker and the person as citizen models unable to support an appropriate moral response of individuals, the same is true of the moral response of communities in social emergencies when our understood duties and our intended outcomes are beyond our reach and we require some new response to the realities that surround us.

In place of these two models, Niebuhr proposes the model of the person as answerer. The moral agent is attentive to what is going on around her, interpreting the actions of other individuals as well as nature and human institutions and forms of life. And, of course, interpreting what God is doing in the world. She, the moral actor, aspires to do what is fitting, in answer to the acts of others and in answer to the responses of others to her answers. She acts, always in community, always alert and responsive to what is going on. Niebuhr summarizes his idea of this pattern of responsibility as "the idea of an agent's action as response to an action upon him in accordance with his interpretation of the latter action and with his expectation of response to his response; and all this is in a continuing community of agents."[26]

---

26. Niebuhr, *Responsible Self*, 65.

We may well wonder about the act of interpretation that Niebuhr places front and center in the moral life, about how we know what is going on in the world and about how we should discern what answer is appropriate, what answer is fitting to what God is doing in the world. How can we avoid being lost in what we should do and be? "Remember who you are and whose you are," Niebuhr might answer, "and act in that awareness." This wondering about what we are to be and do, this attentiveness to our world and our lives, Niebuhr contends, expresses our moral agency and our understanding of ourselves, and the Christian church is not without resources in aiding our interpretation and understanding.

Put Down the Phone: For Further Thought

1. Identify some person whom you admire. Why do you admire that person? What traits of character or virtues do you admire in the person? Why? Why do you think it good, or right, or fitting for him or her to have this character?

2. Try to identify at least five of your *projects*. How can you tell that these are genuine projects of yours? Are any of these *ground projects*? If not, can you identify any of your *ground projects*? Do you think there is some good or right or fitting number of ground projects in proportion to ordinary or common projects? Why?

3. Christians sometimes speak of their "vocation" or "calling" and believe that one's vocation or calling should be among one's ground projects. Does this idea make sense to you? Why is it a "calling"? Does one have to be a Christian, or at least a theist, a believer in God, in order for it to be intelligible for one to have his or her calling or vocation among his or her ground projects?

4. What might we find troubling about the claim that we are much less products of our own authorship or creation than we usually think? If this is true, does this mitigate our responsibility to become who we should become? If this is true, does this make intellectual mush of the claim that we have a responsibility to become who we should become?

5. What might a poor or bad narrative of a life look like?

6. What do you think H. R. Niebuhr would identify as the places in the world where God is active today? How do you think he would advise you to be responsive, to answer to God's actions, in these places?

3

BEING CHRISTIAN

The aim of this book is to help readers find their way, to help readers become a little less lost, on the journey of living a good life, especially as Christians understand a good life. When it comes to living well, it isn't easy to find one's way, especially to find the way that is right for you or me in light of our identities, in light of the story we tell about ourselves. This book is not exactly the Uber or Lyft of good-life thinking, but we do want to help folks think better about the good life and to live well in light of who they are. Many readers may think that even this relatively modest aim is an impossible dream, for, they assume, each of us has her own individual good life. They assume that each of us has a unique, or at least pretty different, understanding of what is good and how we should and shouldn't live. There is no "good life" even for Christians as a group, they may claim. As Sly and the Family Stone sang many years ago, in a song that to this day rewards listening, "Different strokes for different folks (and so on and so on and scooby dooby do wah)."

This may surprise you, but I think the "scooby dooby do wah" the stronger part of Sly and the Family Stone's claim, for, upon closer inspection, there is quite a bit more to be said about what a good life looks like than just "different strokes for different folks." We humans tend to have much more in common than we usually recognize. We shouldn't find it terribly surprising to discover that, in many respects, living well may look much the same for most people. That is what we discovered earlier when we considered believing well. The duties and obligations we have by virtue of being rational creatures don't vary that much from person to person. We have epistemic duties to try not to believe what is false or likely to be false and to try to use reliable methods for acquiring beliefs. Ducks, unlike other humans, don't have the same epistemic obligations you and I have, although like us they can enjoy a fine day by the lake.

So it is, also, with our moral or ethical duties and obligations. Almost all humans agree that "because I want to" and "because I feel like it" are not sufficient reasons for doing significant harm to another person. Almost all humans agree that we should try to keep our word to at least some people, although we may differ about exactly to whom, that is, to which people, we have that obligation. Social psychologist Jonathan Haidt has developed what he calls "Moral Foundations Theory" to explain the rather impressive agreement across cultures on our moral obligations and duties not to harm, to be fair, to be loyal, and to recognize legitimate authorities.[1] And this much agreement should not surprise us, for these moral obligations regulate our lives together and in order to live together peaceably, we must recognize and adhere to at least some obligations like these.

But, despite what we have in common in some of our basic beliefs and commitments in rationality and in morality, when we move beyond the basics, we do find differences. Many of these differences can be explained by what individuals care about and how we have oriented ourselves to what we believe to be good. In the last chapter we saw that to be somebody is to have an identity made up of desires, emotions, tastes, affections, habits, beliefs, loves, and cares. And we saw that tracing the origin of many of these in our lives is no easy task. Who we are is some mixture of genetics, nature, and our environment; the nurture of our parents and families; and the institutions and communities in which we have been nurtured and raised. And we should add to that our own individual contributions, whatever the sources of those contributions—who we have tried and are trying to become and be in light of what we care about. And this is where religious belief, religious attitudes, religious practices, and religious cares and commitments come in. Despite how much Christians (and other religious believers) may have in common with others in what they believe to be true and good, they also see the world differently from many others, and love and care for different things, and have different ground projects than those who do not share their faith.

And this is to say that although there is a great deal of overlap in what Christians and others who are not Christians recognize as their epistemic and moral obligations and in what they think a life well lived may look like, they have different loves, different motivations, different cares and

1. Haidt, *Righteous Mind*, 131–79.

commitments and ground projects because of how their faith makes sense of the world. Although Christians and others inhabit the same world, it may not always look the same, and they may inhabit that world differently because of who they are and how they see the world, because of their identities and the role of faith or its absence in those identities.

3.1 CHRISTIAN IDENTITY AND THE EXPERIENCE OF GOD

In the next several chapters I am going to describe what I take to be at the core of *Christian* identity or *Christian* self-understanding. I am going to try to unpack how Christians understand themselves and how they see the world in light of their experience of God. I assume that much of what I say will be obvious to many who call themselves Christians, but others may not have thought much about it at all. If you call yourself a Christian, I hope this picture of Christian experience will look familiar and true to you. To the extent that it doesn't, at least one of us—and maybe *both*—misunderstands how Christians do and should think of their experience of God.[2] If you are spiritual but not religious, or if you are not spiritual but are interested in better understanding Christians, I hope this will help in that endeavor and that perhaps you can mine what is here for your own self-understanding.

It is unlikely, just from seeing two people walking down a street, that you would be able to identify whether one of the two persons thinks of herself as Christian and, thus, as one who includes among her wants and desires or cares the project of living and acting as a Christian. There are no Christian ways of walking, no definitive Christian symbols (certainly not the cross, at least not since the pop singer Madonna's popularization of crosses as accessories in the mid-eighties), no universal Christian style of dress, no halos over our heads, not even a special twinkle in the eyes.[3] We might wonder, then, exactly what makes one a Christian. Is it some set of statements a person believes—to be a Christian is to believe X and Y, but

---

2. I offer this not as a "descriptive" account of Christian experience, confirmable by an empirical survey of those who identify with the Christian faith tradition. Rather, this is an attempt at a *normative* explanation, an account of what Christian thinkers (or, at least, this Christian thinker) who have studied the Christian Scriptures and the teaching of the Christian church throughout the centuries have articulated as the core Christian experience.

3. But what about tattoos? Arguably, tatts may be better evidence. But often Christian tattoos are not easily seen or recognized and, of course, much as my tattoo of Lenore may tell you something about who I once loved, so a tattoo of a cross or a Bible verse may tell you only that at one point in time that was a major love of mine.

perhaps not Z? Is it some set of dreams, aspirations, and hopes, a way of looking and seeing the world and its future? Is it a set of practices that all Christians engage in? Is it a person's projects and priorities, how a person tries to live, what she intends to do and what she tries not to do? Is it how a person feels about certain things?

Each of these—beliefs, vision, practices, projects and actions, and affections—is an essential component of Christian identity. To be a Christian is, indeed, to believe certain things (and to believe other things to be false), to see the world a certain way and to hope for a future, to join with others in certain common practices like confessing sin and partaking of the body and blood of Christ in Communion, the Eucharist. It is also a matter of doing certain things (and refraining from doing other things) and a matter of cares, of loving and, perhaps, even hating some things.

Some of these are aspects of one's *experience of God*, while others *result from* such an experience. That is to say, one cannot experience God in the absence of some beliefs and affections. Other beliefs, affections, and actions normally follow from an experience of God. Those who believe God does not exist will have no conscious experience of God so long as they hold that belief. (Of course, the unbeliever may abandon her unbelief in the presence of an unbidden appearance of God to her.) And there may be some people whose self-loathing is so great that it precludes them from believing that God genuinely loves them. Some people might hate themselves so much that they believe a perfect God couldn't love something so imperfect and worthless as they are. So, at the outset, what one believes and how one feels may make a big difference for one's experience of God and *whether* one experiences God, and in these respects the experience of God is quite similar to our experience of lots of other things, like donuts and dogs and good books. If you think there is no such thing as a good book, or you simply don't like books, even good books, then you are very unlikely to read one.

Fundamental to being a Christian, to understanding oneself as a follower or disciple of Christ, are experiences that both ground and enrich a person's beliefs about herself and God and that provide a new way of seeing and hoping. These experiences encourage some (and discourage other) ways of acting, and are the basis for certain feelings rather than others. To understand how Christians understand living a good life, then, we first need some sense of Christian experience, some sense of what Christians think and feel about the world and our place in it and how we are to live before God in light of our encounters with God.

At the heart of Christian experience is an encounter that leads to a movement, a shift, in one's identity, what has been described as a movement *from the world to Christ*. What does it look like and feel like to encounter

God as Christians know God, a meeting with a person "Other" than those we meet in our normal everyday experience? How do one's encounters with God affect one's encounters with the world, thus making a difference for Christian living? What does it look like, having encountered God, to understand oneself in a process of moving *from the world to Christ*?

Of course, Christians claim to encounter God in many different ways and in many different times and places. Christians meet God in daily "quiet times" and in Sunday morning worship. Christians see the face of God in children, in the weak and vulnerable, and trace the hand of God in a sunset, a majestic mountain range, and a snowflake. Sometimes I am alone when God meets me, and no one else can know what that meeting with God is like. At other times, I am in a group of Christians and we are all speaking the same words to God, and God is speaking to us in words that anyone can hear. If we abstract from these many and varied encounters with God some core features of the Christian experience of God, what do we find?

The core Christian experience, the experience of God around which, in some way, all other experiences of God revolve, involves some mixture and interpenetration of the perception that the world is a wonderful, glorious place, that things in the world are not the way they should be, and that God is for us and the world God has created. Together, the sense of a world of wonder, a world that is broken, and that God is for us and all that God has created moves us from the wonderful, yet broken, world to Christ. The order of these perceptions of God and the world may vary from person to person. Life is so hard for some folks that God must shock them into seeing the beauty of our lives, while for others the shock is that, in fact, things are not the way they are meant to be. For some, an awareness of God's goodness and God's gift of grace precedes the awareness that our world is messed up. For others, an awareness of God's goodness and kindness is experienced first as a response to humans and how messed up things are.

Still, the foundational experience, whatever the order of the perceptions of the world and God, and however these perceptions interpenetrate one another, is the experience of *guilt*, understood broadly as the recognition that we humans are complicit in the world's not being what God the Creator wants for the creation; the experience of *grace*, understood broadly as *God for us* in creating a marvelous universe and intending goodness and beauty for humans and the universe and in coming to us and acting in Jesus Christ to achieve the goodness and beauty that God intends for the universe; and an experience of *gratitude*, understood as an appreciation and love for God, for God's loving intentions and action for God's creation. Grace and gratitude, then guilt; or guilt and gratitude, then grace—experiences may vary. What is constant is the awareness of the world's need for God (including one's own condition of need before God), the awareness of the beauty and goodness of God's creation, an awareness intensified, perhaps, by the discovery of God's response in Christ to the world's need and the need that characterizes the human condition, and a response of gratitude to the love that will not let us go.[4] To put it simply, *Christians are those who, aware of the world's goodness and the world's great need, including their own great need, experience God's gracious and forgiving love and respond to that gracious love with gratitude to God.* We inhabit a world we recognize as good, we experience godly *grace* in the gift of Christ, and we respond to this gift of God's goodness with *gratitude* and love for God.[5] The core Christian experience is an encounter with the God who reveals to us that God is *for us* and has ever been *for us* and *for God's creation* and who calls us to follow God away from the broken world to the world the loving God desires. Living well for Christians, then, is first and foremost a response to the action God takes of meeting us in Christ and showing love *for us* and *for the world.* But this is too cold and abstract; let's see if we can't paint the picture with more vivid colors. What does the Christian believe about herself and the world (or what does she come to believe about herself and the world) in her encounter with God?

3.2 ASPECTS OF THE CHRISTIAN EXPERIENCE OF GOD: THINGS AREN'T THE WAY THEY'RE MEANT TO BE

Although it is not unique to them, common to all Christians and their experience of the world is a sense of there being something wrong with the world, of things being awry and not the way they are supposed to be.[6] "Something is wrong here!" is a foundational Christian insight, even if not uniquely Christian. The moment in Christian experience at which this is recognized is not uniform. Some people are first struck by the beauty, generosity, and goodness of God. These people may love God deeply before

---

4. This is not to maintain that this is a single, discrete experience of God. This experience may be distilled from a variety of more complex encounters with God over a wide span of time.

5. Again, in describing this experience as *foundational*, I do not mean to suggest that this is the first experience one is conscious of having with the God who knit us together and knew us in our mother's womb. This experience is foundational in the sense that one's experience and understanding of oneself as a Christian properly assume this experience (or one very much like it).

6. Stephen Prothero observes that although they may understand what is wrong with the world in significantly different ways, all religions do share the belief that something is significantly wrong with the world. See his *God Is Not One.*

they sense the depth of evil and ugliness in the world. In fact, it may be that they observe wickedness in the world only because they have first tasted and seen the goodness of God. Other people, however, respond to God's love precisely because of its contrast with the way they believe the world is. Having seen wickedness and great wrongs in the world, they look for goodness and find a sure relief in God. Sooner or later, however, Christians recognize that things in the world aren't as they should be.

The exact content and character of this sense of something being wrong in the world likewise differs from Christian to Christian and from place to place and time to time. Central to the moral thought of ancient Greek philosophers like Socrates and Plato was the view that there are two fundamental problems in the world. First of all, the very stuff of visible reality is inferior and second-rate. We really shouldn't expect much of a material world, for changeable matter is less real and less good than unchangeable spirit.[7] The second problem is human ignorance; we humans just don't know everything we need to know in order to live well in our world. We get lost and we go wrong because we don't know what we need to know in order to choose rightly and well, and we choose poorly without the requisite knowledge.

Christians throughout the ages have found both of these views most tempting, even though neither is easily squared with what the Christian Scriptures say and what the church has taught about God and human nature. A perfectly good and powerful God has created a *good* universe, not a second-rate universe. The story of creation in Genesis displays to us a God who creates and, having created, delights in creation because God sees that it is very good (Gen 1:31), not a God who creates and then says, "Well, pretty good, I guess, all things considered," or "Not too bad, given the materials I had to work with." In contrast, a sense that things are misdirected, out of sync, and out of order with what God hopes and intends for the creation, is central to a Christian understanding of persons and the world in which we live. This perception, this belief and its accompanying feeling,[8] is a starting point for Christians grasping their need and the world's need for God. It is the cornerstone of Christian experience.

Cornelius Plantinga Jr. has illustrated this point with an example from the film *Grand Canyon*.[9] An attorney in an expensive car attempts to escape

7 This outlook is pretty clearly (and somewhat winsomely) articulated in Plato's *Phaedo* and his *Timaeus*.

8. Could one have the belief that things are not the way they should be and lack its appropriate emotional counterpart? Or would the absence of the appropriate feeling indicate some defect of the belief about sin and evil in the world?

9. Lawrence Kasdan's 1991 film is still worth viewing, and Cornelius Plantinga Jr.'s *Not the Way It's Supposed to Be: A Breviary of Sin* is still worth reading.

a traffic jam by driving through a deserted and dangerous part of a city. His car stalls, and before the tow truck he has called arrives to help him, he is confronted by a gang of kids who threaten both his life and his car. When the tow truck driver pulls up to assist the attorney, the kids are angry at the driver's interference. The tow truck driver pulls the gang leader aside and explains, "Man, the world ain't supposed to work like this. Maybe you don't know that, but this ain't the way it's supposed to be. I'm supposed to be able to do my job without askin' you if I can. And that dude is supposed to be able to wait with his car without you rippin' him off. Everything's supposed to be different than what it is here." The horrendous devastation wreaked by AIDS, cyclones, and famines in Africa and Asia; tribal wars fought with weapons supplied by the wealthy; the worldwide refugee crisis; global climate change and environmental destruction; poverty, neglect, and shootings in America's cities; racism; sexism and the oppression of women; terrorism; political instability and unrest; child abuse and slavery—this is not the way the world should be. This is not the world as God wants it to be. Something—somewhere, somehow—has gone terribly wrong. This insight, this deep awareness that the world is filled with struggle and strife, with anger and hatred, *but that it ought not to be* is the starting place for many in their encounter with God, an awareness often heightened by the awareness of the grandeur and beauty and goodness of the world—at times.

3.3 ASPECTS OF THE CHRISTIAN EXPERIENCE OF GOD: WE AREN'T THE WAY WE'RE SUPPOSED TO BE

For some Christians, this primary sense of wrong in the universe is accompanied by a perception of themselves as individuals failing in some way to measure up, failing to meet the standard appropriate to them.[10] They fall short in meeting the standard of goodness and godliness.[11] They locate

---

10. The distinction between these Christians and Christians who focus less upon their own shortcomings even while admitting that things are not the way they are supposed to be is very roughly that made by William James (following Francis W. Newman) between the "twice-born" and the "once-born" or between the "morbid-minded" and the "healthy-minded" Christians. For his rich discussion, see James, *Varieties of Religious Experience*, lectures iv–vii.

11. It is a matter of some significant theological dispute just how accurate the sinner's knowledge of her own sin can be. Some—the melancholy Dane Søren Kierkegaard, for example, and that twentieth-century theological giant, Karl Barth—maintain that the "natural" mind could never really know the nature and extent of sin. Sin blinds us and prevents us from seeing, as well as wanting to see, the nature and extent of our

what's wrong in the universe as not only "out there" but also "in here," in their own actions or thoughts. Not only is something out of sync in the universe, something is out of sync within themselves (and the two are not unrelated). "Something is significantly wrong with *me*, with what I'm doing or with what I am," they think. "I am not as good as I should be, as the world needs me to be; I am not as good as God desires me to be."

Even here, there are important differences among those who confess the name of Christ. For some, a recognition of their own guilt and short-comings precipitates a self-loathing and self-hatred, an emotional sickness, incompatible with the love of God for them. Others resist the despair that some mistakenly find in their guilt. Some find their fault in the contrast between their own character and the character of God; they have met a holy, righteous God, a perfect Being, before whom they can but tremble. Or they know God's will, and the law of God is clear to them, but they do not adequately love and obey the God who commands. Their thoughts and deeds like "filthy rags," they can but hope that God will wash them "whiter than snow." "God be merciful to me, a poor, miserable sinner, unworthy to eat even the crumbs which might fall from your perfect banqueting table." The words of the hymn "Jesus, Lover of My Soul," by the eighteenth-century hymnist Charles Wesley (1707–88), capture well this sense of unworthiness, of not being who and what God wants one to be:

> Just and holy is Thy Name,
>   I am all unrighteousness;
> False and full of sin I am,
>   Thou art full of truth and grace.

Other Christians find this view of a holy and mighty law-giving God, standing over against and judging human behavior, quite appalling; God

---

sin; God must show it to us. (One strain of Christian thought maintains that we can bear to see neither the real nature and extent of our evil nor the real nature and extent of God's goodness.) To claim otherwise, Barth thought, is to minimize the centrality of Christ for the moral and religious life. Thus, Barth writes that "only when we know Jesus Christ do we really know that man is the man of sin, and what sin is, and what it means for man" (*Church Dogmatics*, IV/1, 389).

This is a difficult issue. Can one really know Jesus Christ without knowing why the world needs him? Or is it the case that one can never really know how and why the world needs him until one understands who and what Jesus is and has accomplished? Perplexing! Nevertheless, I think most Christians would claim that having encountered God in Jesus, they see the world in a way they previously could not have, and thus see the nature and gravity of their sin only then (if even then). For our purposes, it is enough to say that, however inaccurate our knowledge of human sin prior to our encounter with Christ, we know enough and our knowledge is accurate enough to rightly convince us of our sin before God.

comes to us as Love, not as all-powerful Legislator and Judge. Still, these other Christians may recognize that they themselves do not love as Love would have them love, do not achieve all they think they ought to, that they are not worthy of the love so generously offered to them. The "fat, relentless ego," as the twentieth-century British philosopher Iris Murdoch puts it, dogs their every thought and action.[12] The good they know they should do they do not do (Rom 7:16–19), for it is hard, oh so hard, to be kind to the village idiot on a Monday morning, or to write even one more letter about world hunger. A harsh word, a missed opportunity to support one's spouse or children, looking the other way in the presence of wrong—these are the day-in, day-out realities of our lives. Deep within us, our consciences testify that even if we are not all that bad, we are not really all that good. We could do better and we should do better. Philosopher Christian Miller describes this as "the character gap."[13] Although we are not as bad, as evil as we might be, neither are we nearly as good as we should be. There is a gap between our actual moral characters and virtuous moral character.

The differences between these two perceptions of what is wrong with our world and with ourselves ought not to be minimized; an emphasis on one's widely missing God's mark may lead to a much different theology than an emphasis on one's missing a natural human mark and then turning to God for help.[14] But the fact remains that both these types of Christians recognize not only that the world is not what it is supposed to be but also that we are not (yet) what God wants us to be, and they admit a need for God in the face of suffering and wrongdoing; both are aware of humans falling short or missing the mark of what we should be and do in the world. We need God because things in the world are messed up; we are not the sorts of folks the world is supposed to have. Our world needs better humans.

All is not well—with us or with the world; this is the belief that lies at the heart of the individual's turn from the world to Christ and to the God Christians worship.[15] The world needs fixing and so do we humans. But we

12. Murdoch, *Sovereignty of the Good*, 52.

13. Miller, *Character Gap*, xi.

14. Author Garrison Keillor has frequently observed the theological implications of these different positions in his contrasts of the "dark Lutherans" with the "happy Lutherans." See, for example, *Wobegon Boy*.

15. Again, I do not mean to claim that for each and every Christian the starting point in the turn to God is always exactly this belief. Some Christians may begin their journey with an overwhelming sense of the goodness of life or the presence of God, with the constant assurance of God's loving care conveyed through their exchanges with God in worship, a steady awareness and perception of the divine presence rather than an awareness of a significant absence in the world. My claim is, however, that even these Christians must make their way through the gate of a conviction of a muddled

cannot fix it. Love, sweet love won't do the trick of fixing what is wrong with the world, though Love Itself might—thus the human turn from the world to God, source of all being, source of healing of the ills that beset us and trouble our world.

Of course, this turn to God may be but a sign of weakness. Christians could just be emotionally unstable people, weaklings unable to live comfortably in a world that frequently disappoints us. Masters of self-hatred (as the nineteenth-century German philosopher Friedrich Nietzsche seemed to think), maybe we Christians feel *guilt* when *shame* for our self-created and imposed fragility would be more appropriate. Maybe Christians, emotional weaklings in a tough, hard world, invent Christianity as a crutch to lean on for support. Maybe the best advice one could give Christians is "Hey, get a life! So, reality bites. What's new?"

While this may be good advice for some few Christians, it is not the response favored by Christianity's more cultured despisers. Most people, the nonreligious as well as the religious, readily agree that all is not well with the world. Many, if not most, would identify human mischief and wrongdoing as the source of most of what is wrong in the world, although, as we have noted, they might disagree as to the cause of human mischief and wrongdoing. Indeed, the great American theologian Reinhold Niebuhr (brother to H. Richard Niebuhr, whom we met in the last chapter) opined that there was but one empirically verified Christian doctrine. The only doctrine we can know to be true by observing the world around us is the doctrine of original sin, the Christian teaching that humans have an ineradicable proclivity to do harm to themselves and to each other and to the world in which we live. Few folks can be found who contest the basic Christian sense that there is something badly wrong with us and with the world. Those who have thought carefully about Christianity and have rejected Christian faith as a way of life typically reject Christian faith on other grounds, not on the grounds that Christians are deeply mistaken in our perception that things are not the way they ought to be.

What marks the Christian is the move she makes given her perception of the world and herself needing fixing and improvement. One might grasp the wretchedness of the world, the inhumanity of humans to other humans as well as human hostility to the world around us, and sink into despair— just give up on things.[16] What sense can we make of the way things are?

---

and messed-up world if they are to journey to the God confessed by Christians. Things are not the way they are supposed to be, with the world or with us.

16. Indeed, philosophers who follow in the footsteps of the seventeenth-century French philosopher Blaise Pascal believe that despair is the only rational alternative to belief in God. See, for example, Pascal's "Wretchedness," in *Pensées*, 44–50.

Chance happens, and with chance, evolution, and with evolution, a world with things not quite the way we might like them to be. What does it matter, given that we have no control over how things will turn out? We can't change the way things are, so why bother trying? This world is a sad place indeed.

Or, instead of despairing, one might respond with a stiff upper lip, buck up and endure our frequently sad world.[17] So things are not the way they are supposed to be; it has always been that way. We march on, carrying the torch for future generations, that they might create a better world until the day evil is eradicated or until we die.

By contrast, what marks the Christian is her renunciation of the world as it is rather than the world as God means for it to be. In turning to God, she turns away from a broken world. She can no longer live in peace in a world of such evil, of such harm done to God's creation and to those created in God's image, so she turns away from the world and turns to God. And, following this turn from the world to God, what marks the Christian is her conviction that Jesus Christ, God yet human, entered human history precisely in order to address this problem of the wrongs and evils in the world. *God came to earth to make right what had gone wrong, to accomplish God's aims for God's creation, and Jesus is the God who has made right and will yet someday make fully right all that is wrong in us and in all of God's creation. God came to earth to heal.* That is the fundamental confession of Christians in the face of the evil in the world.

This claim about Jesus as the one who has come to put things right is not pulled out of thin air. In fact, it is important to be clear about its origins. This claim that God has done something radically new in Jesus makes sense to Christians as part of a story about God conveyed in the narrative, laws, poetry, and wise sayings collected and preserved as the Bible (the Holy Scriptures of Christians) by the Christian church. Christians would not confess what they do about Jesus the Christ were it not for the Bible's story and their hearing God speak to them in the Bible. Christians recognize as true and authoritative the story of God recorded and preserved in the Christian Scriptures and protected by the Christian church. Christians believe that the God they have encountered, the God who created a good

---

17. There are, of course, other strategies of coping as well. Pascal mentions the strategy of *diversion*, of not permitting oneself to face the reality of our condition in the world. Popular American diversions include work, sex, sports, and money. Other strategies more suited to the American temperament include the now popular strategy of worshipping a god of one's own making who may assure the believer that things with him really aren't nearly so bad as they seem. See, for example, Jeremiah Creedon's "God with a Million Faces," 42, as well as Wuthnow, *After Heaven*, and Christian Smith, *Souls in Transition*.

and beautiful world, the God who has sustained that good world despite its failure to be what it was meant to be, the *God for us and for God's creation* is the God who has radically intervened in human history in Jesus. God has come to us in Jesus in order to heal, to restore and re-create the world, to make all things new. This is the God Christians believe they have met, the One whose story the Bible tells.

Esther John (Qamar Zia) (1929–60)

All we like sheep have gone astray; we have all turned to our own way, and the LORD has laid on him the iniquity of us all. (Isa 53:6)

Founded in 960 AD, and built in stages over the centuries, London's Westminster Abbey is now more than eight hundred years old. The last major work on the Abbey was completed in 1745 with Nicholas Hawksmoor's design for the western towers. In 1995, the two western towers were restored. Following the restoration, ten statues were added above the entrance in memory of the lives of Christians who had no special relation to Britain or to the Abbey. These ten modern martyrs, from countries near and far, had suffered for their love of God and for their love of their neighbors. They are remembered not only for their own sacrifices but also as representatives of the Christians throughout the world who have suffered, and the many who still, to this day, suffer persecution. Well-known twentieth-century Christian saints like Martin Luther King Jr., Óscar Romero, and Dietrich Bonhoeffer stand above the entrance. Next to Bonhoeffer stands Esther John, born Qamar Zia.

Qamar Zia was born into a relatively affluent Muslim family in Madras (now Chennai), India, in 1929, one of seven children. As a teenager, she was enrolled in a nearby Christian school when her father became ill. At this school she was first introduced to the Christian Scriptures, and she was taken by the kindness of her teachers. Although, at first, she had little interest in reading the Bible, that slowly changed. After reading the words of Isaiah 53 and seeing Jesus in the Song of the Suffering Servant, Qamar quietly yet courageously converted to the Christian faith. Her conversion was her secret, a secret not shared with her traditional Muslim family.

In 1947, she and her family moved from India to the city of Karachi, in the newly independent state of the Islamic Republic of Pakistan. In Karachi, she was befriended by Marian Laugesen, a Christian missionary, who had been alerted by one of Qamar's school teachers in Madras that Qamar's family had moved to Karachi and was living in the refugee community there. Laugesen found Qamar and in meeting with her to teach her English, she surreptitiously gave Qamar a copy of the New Testament. Qamar secretly read the New Testament, without instruction, for the next seven years. All this time, Laugesen prayed for her.

In her mid-twenties, fearing that her parents would arrange a Muslim marriage for her and that she would be forced to abandon her Christian faith, Qamar ran away from home, fleeing first to the orphanage where Marian Laugesen was a teacher. There she took her new name, Esther John. But Esther was torn, loving her Muslim family very deeply but loving the God she had met in Jesus even more. After a very brief stay, she hurried to Sahiwal, hundreds of miles away, to a mission hospital, where she was baptized. At the hospital, she lived openly as a Christian, in a Christian community, serving others in the hospital as she prepared to be a teacher. After three years of education, she moved to a small country town nearby, from which she frequently traveled by foot and by bicycle to area villages. In these villages, she lived alongside the local women, working with them in the cotton fields, teaching them to read, and sharing her faith in Christ Jesus. In many ways, she was a mystery to these women, unconventional as she was in her dress, in publicly riding her bicycle and in teaching, and, above all, in appearing to have given up her family to become a "low-caste Christian."

Before long, her brothers discovered her whereabouts and pressured Esther to return to their home. Eventually, Esther agreed to return to them, but only after negotiating with them. She finally compromised on where she would live—but not on her faith. She agreed to return to Karachi on the condition that she could live openly as a Christian and that she would not be pressured into marriage. Her family did not respond to her offer of compromise.

Only thirty years old, on February 2, 1960, Esther John was found dead in her house in the country village of Chichawatni, a victim of a violent attack. Her murderer was never identified and her death to this day remains unsolved. The investigators found little evidence—only that, as they put it, "this girl was in love—only with your Christ." She was buried in the Christian cemetery at Sahiwal, where, later, a chapel in her memory was built in front of the hospital where she served.

Esther John's statue now stands above the entry to Westminster Abbey, a model for Christians of loving God with all one's heart, soul, and strength, and a representative of the many faithful and true servants in all countries of the world who, like Esther, have quietly and courageously loved Christ and loved their neighbors as themselves—suffering servants faithful to their God, like the servant spoken of in Isaiah 53, who poured out himself to death (Isa 53:12).[18]

Put Down the Phone: For Further Thought

1. Some painfully graphic examples of things not being the way they are meant to be are the horrendous famines in Yemen and South Sudan, the recent genocide in Darfur, the devastation in Africa caused by AIDS, terrorist attacks across the globe, gigantic oil spills off the Gulf Coast of the United States, global climate change, and mass shootings in schools and churches. How do people who are not Christians make sense of such evils? How do they explain why such things happen and why they matter? How do Christians make sense of such evils? What do you make of these different explanations of evil? Are there better reasons to hold one view on these evils than another? How so?

2. Why would a good God permit horrendous evils? Couldn't an omnipotent (i.e., all-powerful) God prevent horrendous evils? Wouldn't an omni-benevolent (all-loving) God prevent horrendous evils? So how do those who hold a traditional Christian (or monotheistic) view of God explain these evils?

3. Imagine meeting someone who lacked the sense that things aren't the way they're meant to be in any major way. What explanation could you give for someone failing to hold this belief? Could anything be said or argued to bring a person to the belief that things aren't the way they are meant to be?

4. Does it make any sense to talk about "the gravity of sin"? What could this mean? Do you think someone who hasn't recognized the gravity of her own sin can really love and follow God? Why or why not? Do you think someone who hasn't recognized her "soul's worth," her value to God, can love and follow God? Why or why not?

5. What difference should your awareness of evil in the world make for how you live your life? Is this awareness necessarily a motivation to do good? Instead, could it lead to moral paralysis?

6. Can you think of other accounts of the human proclivity to sin that make as much or more sense than the Christian account?

---

18. Esther John's story is told by Janet Ballantyne White, *Esther: Story of a Pakistani Girl*, and by Patrick Sookhdeo, "Mission and Conversion in Pakistan."

7. If what Christians say about sin is true, what does this mean with respect to the ability of those who are not Christians to grasp that truth? What do you think the implications are of this view of sin for whether those who are not Christians can live a good life?

8. Are you surprised that Esther John's statue appears alongside of Christian martyrs like Martin Luther King Jr., Óscar Romero, and Dietrich Bonhoeffer? Make a case for and against including her in this group.

4

GOD'S STORY AND OUR STORY

St. Augustine (354–430)[1]

Few, if any, thinkers have influenced Christian thought as much as St. Augustine. His *Confessions* is both stirring autobiography and deeply insightful theology. His *City of God* is a complicated (and very lengthy) exploration of psychology, theology, political theory, and cultural analysis. Each of these books continues to repay frequent rereading for their insight into the human condition and the world in which we live. The same could be said of many more of his works.

Augustine was born in Roman North Africa in 354, the son of a middle-class couple who wanted few things more than to see their son rise in social rank. He was sent to the best schools his parents could afford as he trained to become a teacher of rhetoric. A brilliant student, along the way he made his way through several non-Christian religions and philosophies, discovering their strengths and their shortcomings, as they led to his turning from the world to Christ and his conversion in 386. Following this conversion, he had hoped to establish a monastery where he and several like-minded friends would pursue a life of reflection upon Christian faith. But, instead, he was called into the service of the church at Hippo, a community of Christians whom he served

---

1. This material on Augustine is derived from my "Habit's Harsh Bondage."

for the next forty years of his life, first as a priest and later, at their insistence, as their bishop.

In his mid-forties, near the turn of the fifth century, Augustine began writing his *Confessions*. Modern readers may expect from the title an explicit and lurid account of an endless number of sexual trysts, a Christian "tell-all" sex romp. But that is not what they find. Garry Wills suggests that a better title for the book is *The Testimony*, for Augustine's aim is not to confess but rather to give testimony and praise to the God he has encountered in Christ Jesus.[2] Although Augustine is profoundly concerned about his own sexual history and explicit in recounting his past, modern readers are unimpressed by his exploits. His sexual sins strike us as mere peccadilloes, hardly worthy of getting worked up over by our modern standards. Yet his insight into the sway his sexual appetites held over him is central to his understanding of sin and evil and crucial to his testimony to the goodness and power of God. He was convinced that things in himself and in the world are not the way they are supposed to be and that healing and hope lay in his turning from the world to God.

According to Augustine, Adam and Eve, the first humans, were originally obedient to God, their true and rightful superior. Their individual natures (like all things in the world) were correctly ordered and properly functioning. Their loves were directed appropriately to the being and value of each person and thing. Originally, they loved the animals they had named and they loved one another fittingly, with a love that was proportionate to the value of the other. All was well with the world. But then they rebelled against God, they rejected God's creation and ordering of creation and the true value of God and the things created by God. In so doing they invited disorder into the universe and into their lives. As C. S. Lewis once put it, "Man has called for anarchy: God lets him have it."[3]

Before Adam and Eve sinned, there was a unity and an order to our (human) internal workings, to our willings, and thinkings, and feelings, and doings, our cares and projects. But the fall—the rebellion against God and, thus, the introduction of sin into the world in the disobedience of Adam and Eve—has changed that, Augustine argued. Now, post-fall, our passions are no longer obedient to the proper control of reason, just as our reason is no longer obedient to God. For Augustine, our sexual passions provide one of the clearest displays of distorted and

2. Wills, *Saint Augustine's Childhood*, 13–15.
3. Lewis, *Preface to Paradise Lost*, 69–70.

disordered human nature after the fall. Hence, Augustine's "preoccupa-tion" with sex. Sexual activity, originally created as a good thing with its own purposes, is now messed up, not the way it is supposed to be. Messed up sex, bad sex, hurts us and hurts those we care about.

Augustine thought that when we honestly examine our sexual desires, we discover our conflicted characters. With great frequency, reason tilts us in one direction while sexual desire tugs in another. Thus, we turn to gaze lustfully at another person when we know we shouldn't. Things we believe we ought not to find at all pleasurable we find erotic and sexually stimulating. We discover that sexual arousal is out of our control; sometimes we are unable to function sexually when we want to; sometimes we find ourselves sexually aroused when we would rather not be. The same could be said for other physical desires or passions, of course—for hunger or sleep, for anger and envy. Not just our physical desires but all our wants, all our desires and loves, misfire. We humans are disordered, malfunctioning, and unable to will and to do what God intends for us.

Seen in this light, Augustine's deep concern about his sexual activ-ity is a part of his testimony to the disordered loves that characterized his life, and the disordering of loves that characterizes our lives as well. His reflections upon his sex life are integral to a narrative in which he travels from the world to Christ, from dividedness and disorder to unity and integration. As a sinner, when he looks inward, into himself, he finds a divided self: a self somewhat willing to serve God, as well as a self willing not to serve God. "So I was in conflict with myself and was dissociated from myself. The dissociation came about against my will. Yet this was not a manifestation of an alien mind but the punishment suffered in my own mind."[4] But that fragmentation is not the end of the story. Book Two of *The Confessions*, in which Augustine begins to detail how he formed his sexual habits, opens with a testimony to what God has accomplished in him since his turn to Christ: "You gathered me together from the state of disintegration in which I had been fruitlessly divided."[5] Augustine tells his story as a journey from fragmentation to unity, by God's grace.

Not uncommonly for his time and social class, Augustine had a concubine (a common-law wife) from the age of sixteen until he was thirty-one. He was faithful to her, he tells us. She was the mother of his son, and he was terribly distraught when, soon after his conversion

---

4. Augustine, *Confessions*, 148.
5. Augustine, *Confessions*, 24.

to Christianity, she was forced to leave him and return to her home so he might marry someone appropriate to his social status. Why did Augustine think of such a relatively chaste relationship as morally problematic? Because he did not love her "in God," because, no matter how deep his love for her, he didn't love her for the sort of being God had created her to be. And because in that relationship he had developed habits that tied him to satisfying his desire for sexual pleasure in a manner inappropriate for a "philosopher." He could no longer separate his love for his partner from his desire to have her.

In the mid-380s, as was the practice of the day, Augustine's mother, Monica, arranged a marriage for Augustine with a suitable, more socially acceptable, young girl. Augustine's partner, his common-law wife, thus left him forever, returning to her home in Africa. His behavior after she left was, for him, further evidence that he had not loved his first partner rightly or well. As he awaited the coming of age of his bride-to-be, he followed the lead of his sexual appetite—he took up with a new woman rather than control his appetite for sex. He was chained to the flesh, chained by the sexual habits of years, enslaved by his disordered passions.

As a son of Adam, by his own disobedience Augustine had called for anarchy in his life, and God had granted it. His life seemed out of his control, and in the control of his passions and desires. Where self-control is absent, "the desire of the flesh, the desire of the eyes, the pride in riches" (1 John 2:16) are irresistible.

Augustine understood the lust of the eyes to be a type of curiosity, a "vain inquisitiveness" into the look of things, an intense desire just to see things for the thrill of it. This desire is satisfied by the sight of new things, things not yet seen, and is fueled by the promise of different and ever more stimulating views. In his time, the theater was a primary draw for the curious. Lest the curious become sated and jaded with what was on offer, increasingly outrageous events were staged to satisfy this desire to see, to visually experience something new. Augustine himself had overcome his interest in the theater by the time he had reached his forties. Still, he recognized that he was surrounded by "a buzz of distraction," with innumerable things tugging at his attention to come and have a look.[6]

By God's severe mercy, Augustine tells us, the manacles of his habits were broken. He came to see that we all live, and love, divided and fragmented. Unity of self can be restored, he realized, but only through

---

6. Augustine, *Confessions*, 212.

love of God. "O charity, my God, set me on fire. You command conti-
nence; grant what you command, and command what you will."[7] Make
me a single self, so I can love and obey you, O God.

That self-control finally achieved by Augustine was a gift of God,
even as it was a command of God. Augustine had to acknowledge that
he was not in control of his life, that he was a slave to his desires, and
that only God could deliver him from his bondage. He had to recognize
and receive God's love for him and acquire a new desire to love God. He
had to turn from the world and become willing to forsake inappropriate activities and to abandon fixed habits at odds with the love of God.
There was a time, prior to his conversion, when Augustine thought
such control over his sexual desires impossible. But God delivered to
him that gift of self-control and granted him a restored will with which
he might obey God.

Augustine was not naïve. Old habits die hard. He realized that the
chains of habit are more likely to be broken in a community of others also committed to loving God and their neighbors well. Augustine
could confess that he had achieved control over his sexual desires before he began exercising his priestly duties. The example and support of
his friends, no doubt, played a very large role in this.

Even when habits have died, however, they leave their tracks. A
decade and more after his conversion Augustine observed that God
had granted him control over his sexual desires, but he could not claim
that he was no longer subject to temptation. Images, "fixed by sexual
habit," remained stored in his memory and attacked him, sometimes
when he was awake, often when he was asleep. Awake, he was master
of the images, but asleep, they controlled him. Habit's harsh bondage,
again. But God could, and would, someday deliver him from even these
traces of habit. Augustine lived in the hope of that final and complete
deliverance from the chains of all sinful habits. Until that time, prayer
and watchfulness must be the order of the day. "O charity, set us on fire.
Grant what you command and command what you will."

4.1 THE BIBLE AND THE CHURCH

Like Augustine, having encountered God, Christians have discovered
what they believe to be the world's deepest and truest story. They tell this
story about what God has done (and is doing) in the face of things in God's

---

7. Augustine, *Confessions*, 202.

creation not being the way they should be. They tell a story about God coming to the world as a human, Jesus of Nazareth, a story of Jesus living and dying among us and of God raising Jesus from the dead. And they tell a story of Jesus coming again to make all things new. And that story of what God is doing in the world is a story that includes them, too. Having been adopted as God's children through Jesus Christ (Eph 1:5), they now want to live as children of the Light. Christians tell the story of Jesus the Light of the World, God's story, and the world's story.

Not just any and all stories about Jesus are recognized as true and authoritative by Christians, however. The stories you or I might tell about how God has worked in our lives may be edifying to others, but the Christian church does not recognize our stories as "teachings with authority." And that is also the case with stories that could have been told even by people who were Jesus' contemporaries, should some such new stories now come to light. In fact, Christians recognize only a relatively small body of writings as Scripture or *canon*.[8]

At least two different stories can be told of how the Bible, the Christian Scriptures, was formed. One of them, told by historians, goes something like this. What was important for the earliest Christians was teaching and preaching about Jesus of Nazareth. Their faith was focused upon Jesus. His deeds were recounted, his words were remembered, and his life was reflected upon in light of the Jewish Scriptures and in light of the challenges and crises faced by that early Christian community of faith. By the end of the first century, a number of writings by those who had known Jesus or his first disciples were circulating among Christians, with this number expanding in the second century. These writings are included in the New Testament of the Christian Scriptures. They were the documents most important in the life and worship of the early Christians; for this reason, they were collected and distributed to growing communities of Christians. These were the words about Jesus that rang most true to the early Christians, the words of Jesus and his disciples protected and preserved in order to enable the Christian communities to live more faithfully and to endure the challenges put to them by their world.

We should remember that the first Christians were also Jews, so these writings specifically testifying to the life and teaching of Jesus were not the only writings of importance to the first Christians. Israel's Scriptures—law, sacred narratives, and prophecy and poetry which were used in Jewish worship and teaching, that is, in the life and practice of the Jews—were read and

8. "Canon" is derived from the Greek word for "rule" or "norm" and originally referred to the list of the books regarded as authoritative by the Christian church, and later to the books themselves.

studied by Jesus and his early followers. The Jewish Scriptures, referred to by Christians as the Old Testament, evolved much more gradually than the Christian New Testament. By probably around the fifth century BCE, there was a recognized collection of historical narratives, the *Torah,* or law—the books of Moses or the Pentateuch, the first five books of the Bible. Other scriptures were collected as the *Prophets*, and these books were recognized as authoritative, though always in conjunction with Torah, by most of the Jewish people in the second and first centuries BCE. In addition to these two collections, the assortment of books known as the *Writings*—Psalms, Proverbs, and the like—form the remainder of what Christians recognize as the Old Testament, and by the end of the first century AD these writings, too, were accepted as authoritative by the Jewish people.

The Christian Scriptures, the collection of the books of the Christian Old and New Testaments, then, develop from two separate bodies of literature, the latter of which grew through a sometimes more, sometimes less explicit conversation with the former. This literature that was written and collected and that had evolved over a long number of years, literature that was preserved and legitimated because of its importance in the worship and life of the Jewish people as well as the early Christians and also narratives of the life of Jesus and letters of early Christian leaders were placed together. These writings received their final, authoritative status in the fourth and fifth centuries AD when the various communities of the Christian church recognized these books, and only these books, as telling the story of God and God's people in a powerful and authoritative way.

Christian theologians tell no story at odds with the historical account given above, but they take great pains to tell what they believe to be the rest of the story. And the rest of the story is that the Scriptures were not written, collected, and transmitted by Jews and Christians merely as a means of self-preservation, merely for social, political, or even religious reasons; that way of telling it leaves God out. The rest of the story, Christians believe, is that God the Holy Spirit actively engaged the hearts and minds of the Scripture writers, encouraging, prodding, and inspiring them as they wrote and collected these writings. Christians do not believe that God dictated every word of Scripture the way Muslims believe that God dictated the Qur'an, the sacred book of Islam. Instead, the Holy Spirit worked in and with and through the writers in such a way that the words of Scripture are the genuine words of Matthew, or Luke, or Paul, as well as the word of God. The words of the Christian Scriptures were not handed down from heaven, dictated by God, but they are in a very real sense God's word to us. Christians assert, paradoxically, that every word of Scripture was written by some human hand guided by some human mind, and yet also claim that God was never absent in the selection of these words in these books written and preserved for the sake of the world. The Holy Spirit, too, was active in the preservation of these important texts, and in guiding the Jewish community and the early church to recognize these, and only these, texts as canon, or rule of faith. In the Christian Scriptures we have the words that the early church *under the guidance and inspiration of the Holy Spirit* identified as the words that tell most truly and in a most trustworthy manner the story of God. This story informs and grounds the core Christian experience of God.

4.2 THE STORY OF GOD

The primary encounter of the Christian with God is the encounter of two persons—God and a human—each grasping that things in the world are not as they are meant to be. The awareness of God as one who shares our perception that things aren't as they are meant to be, and one who shares our unhappiness and sorrow with the condition of things, and the recognition that God has acted definitively to correct this condition of the world is mediated, or made known to us, by the Christian Scriptures as they have been entrusted to the Christian church and interpreted by the church. "Jesus loves me, this I know, for the Bible tells me so," Christian children sing.

Those Scriptures are, as we have noted, a complex variety of types of literature written over a large number of years and collected many years later. There is danger, no doubt, in simplifying a body of literature so complex. Nevertheless, the church has professed that there is unity here, amidst the diversity of texts. That unity is the story of God and the mighty acts God has performed in order to make things right with God's creation, to correct the wrong, and to accomplish good in our universe. The Christian Scriptures tell of the God who heals the world; the Bible shows God's true character as *God for us*. Here, in a brief summary, is the complicated story the church has found in the Holy Scriptures entrusted to her by God, a drama in four acts.[9]

Act 1, Creation: In the beginning a good and mighty God created the universe

---

9. Richard Hays helpfully summarizes the New Testament story as follows: "The God of Israel, the creator of the world, has acted (astoundingly) to rescue a lost and broken world through the death and resurrection of Jesus; the full scope of that rescue is not yet apparent, but God has created a community of witnesses to this good news, the church. While awaiting the grand conclusion of the story, the church, empowered by the Holy Spirit, is called to re-enact the loving obedience of Jesus Christ and thus to serve as a sign of God's redemptive purposes for the world" (Hays, *Moral Vision of the New Testament*, 193).

and created humans and all living things. This God created all things because "being" is good. To be is better than not to be, so the God of Love creates a universe of things that are. This God created us human beings in God's image, to love us and to enjoy our company. God desired, from the beginning, the flourishing of all the creation, that each created thing would play its fitting role in God's creation. The original creation, then, is a community of God with humans and the created world and of humans with God, with one another, and with the world in which we live. This is *shalom*, the flourishing and fulfilled peace of all things.[10] In conditions of shalom, all things are what God means for them to be; all things do well what they are meant by God to do. Things are fulfilled in fulfilling their vocation, the work or role for which God has created them. God is thus known, first of all, as a good Creator, a God whose creation of the universe is motivated not by any need but by divine love, a God who has purposes in creating the universe. God creates a good universe so that goodness can be known and enjoyed by all that is created.

Act 2, Fall: Humans, although created good by God, freely chose (and continue freely to choose) a lesser good over the greater good of love and faithfulness to God. In that turning away from God we turn to our own devices and desires, and thus introduce sin, harm, and evil into the world. To this day we know the world and ourselves as broken; things are no longer the way they are meant to be. Human sin unleashes mighty powers of evil and disorder upon ourselves and upon our world. Human sin is the disruption, the cause of things not being the way they are supposed to be with ourselves and with our universe. The gravity of the disorder humans introduced into a good world ought not to be minimized. Nothing in creation has been exempt from the effects of sin. Sin is not a one-off thing; it is the wrong that keeps on harming, and the cosmos suffers for it. We humans know ourselves as having a certain proclivity to choose lesser goods or evils rather than the greater goods that are before us. We know ourselves as disrupters of the goodness that God intends for the creation. Deep down within us, we long to be healed. The whole creation groans as it suffers (Rom 8:22).

Act 3, Redemption: In order to restore creation to its original condition of flourishing, the good and loving God, the gracious Creator of all that is seen and unseen, the God who called Abraham and his offspring to be "a blessing to all the nations" (Gen 22:18), becomes human in Jesus of Nazareth, and lives and dies as a human. Jesus of Nazareth is God Incarnate, *God with us and God for us*, God come to win back and heal the world. God has come to us in Jesus to redeem,

10. See Nicholas Wolterstorff's beautiful and incisive discussion of shalom in Boulton, Kennedy, and Verhey, *From Christ to the World*, 251–53.

restore, *and re-create* the world in all its goodness. In God's call to Israel and in the life, cross, death, and, above all, the resurrection of Jesus, God has begun a new creation. Christians, the followers of Jesus, having heard the message of Jesus to repent and follow him, have turned from the world to Christ. Following Jesus, they turn back toward the world with the outstretched hands of God. The church, the community of those who have recognized God's radical intervention into human history in the life, death, and resurrection of Jesus, is a community called by God to live as first-fruits of the new kingdom and as signposts of the coming completion of God's activity of new creation. Although the promise is made and the guarantee sure, those who now follow Jesus must always struggle to be faithful to the re-creating God in this time prior to the completed re-creation of themselves and God's world. This is the time in which we now live—the time between the beginning of the restoration of all things to God and the completion of God's restorative activity. As such, our lives, the lives of the community of faith in Christ, are characterized by the tension between what God has already begun to accomplish in us and in our world and the restoration that is not yet completed. Followers of Jesus are in the world, but not of the world. Lovers of God, they watch for God's work in the world and respond in faith and hope to what God is doing.

Act 4, Restoration/Re-creation/Fulfillment: God completes the work begun and guaranteed in the life, death, and resurrection of Jesus. What God has promised and what we have anticipated is fully realized. All things are made new. Every tear is dried and all things dwell in harmony with God and with one another (Rev 21:4–5). The disorder of sin is eliminated; things, at last, will be the way they are supposed to be. Shalom is finally realized and enjoyed by all that exists.

4.3 THE STUDY OF GOD AND CHRISTIAN LIVING

Christians are, simply put, persons who respond with gratitude to the God they have encountered in Jesus Christ. The God whose story is told in the Christian Scriptures and told by the Christian church, the God who is the Creator, the Sustainer, and the Redeemer of the universe, the God whose face is shown in Jesus Christ, is the God to whom Christians turn. Having perceived the matchless grace of God, Christians profess their belief in God's projects and commit themselves to these projects, to continuing God's work in the world. They envision the completion of God's story with the world and hope for that day when all shall be well, when things will be the way they are supposed to be. Having come to some understanding of

God's story, Christians wish for their own stories to conform to that story, to be harmonious with God's story, to be taken up into God's story. They aspire to love God well and to rightly and appropriately love other persons and to love God's creation with the right kinds of love.

To put it differently, Christians are pilgrims on a happy journey from their place in a world out of touch and out of sync with God to a world where God and all of God's creation will be known and loved appropriately and well. They don't hate the world from which they turn, a world created good by God, a world with countless beauties, though they do turn from the world and toward God.[11] Having gladly abandoned that place where their hearts were turned away from God and turned in on themselves, Christians believe they are on the road to that place where their love of God, and of other persons, and of all things created by God, will be perfected.

The progress of the Christian toward that holy city is slow and often painful. As she progresses toward that city, the Christian expects her vision of God to become clearer and her love for God to increase. As the ancient hymn has it (a hymn made popular in the musical *Godspell*),

> Day by day, day by day
> Oh, dear Lord, three things I pray:
> To see thee more clearly
> To love thee more dearly
> To follow thee more nearly
> Day by day.[12]

Although the distinction is artificial, one might say that the critical reflection and study aimed at seeing God more clearly is the work of *theology proper* and that the study aimed at loving God more dearly is the study of Christian *spirituality* and *liturgical theology*. The study aimed at helping the Christian pilgrim to follow God more nearly is *Christian ethics, or moral theology*. Of course, we don't carefully carve up our lives into segments of seeing, loving, and following, so this division is artificial. And there is no reason to think one will follow God nearly unless she also sees God clearly and loves God dearly, or that she will see God clearly if she is not following God nearly and loving God dearly. Nor, to be sure, will she love God dearly if she does not see God clearly and follow God nearly. All this is to say

11. Few have been as articulate as St. Augustine in identifying the evils present in our earthly existence. Likewise, few have waxed so eloquently in praising the wondrous beauty of this fallen world. See Boulton, Kennedy, and Verhey, *From Christ to the World*, 234–37.

12. This prayer is attributed to Richard De Wych, St. Richard of Chichester, England (1197–1253).

that if we were going to do things rightly and well, those who would better love God and follow Jesus would study not only Christian ethics but also Christian theology and spirituality/worship, and would study them in some sort of integrated way.[13]

But sometimes dissecting what is unified can bring clarity. And time is short, and there is more than enough material to keep us busy with our focus here upon following Jesus more nearly, of trying to live well, to live a good life, as Christians. This focus upon following God more nearly is something we can do, even if it is not all we should do. We should note as well, however, that as the prayer suggests, these aims of seeing God more clearly, loving God more dearly, and following God more nearly are properly pursued when surrounded by prayer, when supported by prayer. This book, like most works in Christian moral philosophy or moral theology, does not talk much about prayer. That is not because prayer is not important, and not because prayer is not an appropriate subject for critical reflection; it is. But the study of prayer appropriately occurs in theology proper and/or in spirituality/liturgical theology. The study of moral philosophy or theology, the mapping of the contours of a Christian moral life and living well, leaves critical reflection upon the nature of prayer to these other studies.

The practice of prayer, while not the object of our studies, is, nevertheless, a very good thing, and those who care about living well should try to pray often and to pray well. Most of those whose lives I admire, it seems, have admirable prayer lives. Of course, one ought not to pray because it might make one more admirable. (Nor should the fact that *I* admire someone mean that much to you!) But neither should we assume that there is no connection between a heart appropriately turned to God, a prayerful heart, and moral goodness and a life lived well. Properly discerning how we should live, Christians believe, should be directed by God the Holy Spirit, who works in our lives. Even if we aren't very clear about *how* prayer matters for living a good life, Christians assume that prayer does matter. So, by all means, let us pray, even though our work here, in this book, is to critically reflect upon the moral life, broadly construed. Let us pray for God's help, to the end that we might see God more clearly, love God more dearly, and follow Jesus more nearly, in all our days.

---

13. The Anglican moral theologian Kenneth E. Kirk models this understanding of the inseparability of moral theology and "ascetic" theology in his *The Vision of God*. Contemporary Christian ethicists embrace various strategies in order to highlight the connectedness of Christian ethics to theology and liturgics. See, for example, Hauerwas and Wells, *The Blackwell Companion to Christian Ethics*.

Put Down the Phone: For Further Thought

1. Why do Christians believe that the Bible story is true? Can it be proved to be true? What sorts of things, if any, might shake the conviction of Christians that the Bible story is true? Is it rational to believe the Bible story to be true?

2. What does it mean to believe that the Bible story is true? For example, do you believe that the Bible story is true even if you don't believe that God created the universe in six 24-hour days? Do you believe the Bible story even if you're not really sure that Jonah was first swallowed and then spit out by the whale?

3. Are there wrong uses of the Bible story? What would make a use of the story right or wrong?

4. If Christians and Muslims have different beliefs about their holy books and how God speaks and inspires these holy books, does it follow that Christians and Muslims worship a different God?

5. If the Christian life is of one piece, how can ethics be studied without at the same time studying the belief components (theology proper) and the affective components (spirituality/worship) of the Christian faith? Otherwise, aren't we bound to get things wrong?

6. What makes a prayer a *good* prayer? Do we mean a *morally good* prayer? Can a good prayer ever be *morally bad*?

7. How might prayer make a difference for Christian living, for following Jesus? What are some ways that one might study this difference prayer may make?

8. Should one pray to become a good person? Could prayer alone accomplish this?

9. Is prayer just shirking our responsibility to do what we should do?

10. Why should Christians study Christian moral philosophy or theology if they believe that what really matters is whether they are rightly related to God?

11. In what ways do you think St. Augustine used God's story to make sense of his life?

5

FROM CHRIST TO THE WORLD
God's Creation and Value

As we've seen, our identities are complex, sufficiently complex that we can be lost and unclear not only about what is good but about who and what we are. We are what we want, what we love, what we believe, and what we care about, with all of these informing and directing what we do. We tell stories about ourselves to make sense of ourselves; stories that connect our desires, loves, beliefs, and cares; stories that may tell of the unity of our lives, that things do hold together, or stories that sometimes show we are less whole than we would like to be. "That's who I am." Or, sometimes, "I don't know why I did that; that wasn't me. I'm sorry."

Christians locate their stories in a larger story, in God's story. The core Christian experience is the realization that things are not the way they are supposed to be, that we are a part of the old creation that constantly turns away from the never-ending love and grace of God. Nevertheless, despite our refusal to respond appropriately to God and to God's creation, despite our reluctance to love God and to love our neighbor as we should, God loves us. God has intervened in Jesus Christ to heal us and God's whole creation, and to make all things new (Rev 21:1–8). Thus, at the same time that we realize that we are part of the old creation, we realize as well that we are a part of the new creation that God graciously is bringing through Christ Jesus. We discover that, although we have chosen against God, God has chosen *for us* and *for creation*. Our story, we now know, is part of God's story of good news for a creation groaning as it awaits the full and final redemption that is, in Christ, guaranteed.[1]

Our lives, our identities, are transformed and continue to be transformed in our experience of God. Christians profess that our minds—our desires, tastes, affections, emotions, beliefs, and cares—are being renewed (Rom 12:2). We are works in progress. We move from our encounter with God, our experiencing of God, to a new understanding of ourselves (and our world), to a new *identity*. We might think of the change that takes place when one person marries another, when one person publicly commits himself or herself to another as spouse. The new spouse no longer understands himself, or wants to understand himself, as a solitary individual; rather, the world is seen through the lenses of his new identity. "I am Felicia's husband," he thinks. Likewise, the new mother is a new person; she sees and values the world differently, she acquires new ground projects as a result of having a child entrusted to her care. She has new loves. She has new worries and new concerns. She has a new identity. And so it is with Christians, disciples of Christ, followers of God. We see the world and our place in it differently, in a way we would otherwise not see things, in light of our experience of God and God's projects. And we hope to respond to the world differently than how we are tempted to respond to it. We have a new identity. We are new creations.

But what does this new identity of the Christian mean for living a good life, for living well? What does this self-understanding mean for our loves and our cares, for the projects we undertake, including the moral life, that is, for treating others as we ought to? What does a Christian identity mean for who we are to be and what we ought and ought not to do? How is this core Christian experience of the world's not being the way it is supposed to be, the discovery of the goodness and grace of God, and our gratitude to God for the love God shows us and God's creation transformed into a self-understanding that informs and directs how we live? How does one who understands herself as a Christian look at who she should be and what she should do in her life? What do things look like when we shift our attention in the direction of God's attention, back to the world, looking at things through Christian lenses?

---

1. Paul's language in Romans 8:22 is especially vivid. We and the whole universe are somehow aware of the newness coming to birth through God's work in Christ and we groan like a mother giving birth as God makes all things in our universe new. We ought to be mindful that the pain and confusion that is a normal part of childbirth may be a normal part of this new creation's being born.

5.1 GOD, CREATION, AND VALUE

I will suggest what I take to be several of the fundamental implications of Christian identity and understanding for our reflection about living well. I will try to tease out some important foundational assumptions for what and how we should care, and for our ground projects, in the light of the core Christian experience and self-understanding. No doubt, many more things could be said. God's creation abounds with good things, and living well with respect to these goods is complicated. I shall discuss the three theses, three fundamental claims, I take to be most important for grounding our thoughts about how to live—three claims about God and the world, about God's character, and about human nature that follow from the core Christian experience.

> Thesis 1: The created order, the world, has a nature, a character, for it is the creation of a good and loving God. It is a good creation, abundant with objects and experiences that are good and valuable. These goods are worthy of our love, though we often love only apparent goods and mistakenly love real goods poorly and not as we should. God, the Creator, knows what goods are worthy of our love, what kind of love these goods are worthy of, and what ground projects comport with real goods, with God's own loves, and with God's projects and intentions. God judges and acts in accordance with the good that God knows and loves. There are truths about what is good and what is right, about what is of value and worthy of our love, and these truths are not primarily dependent upon us for their status as truths.

5.1.1. God, Goods, and Value: Subjective Value

A perennial issue in philosophy is the question of whether there are truths of the matter about at least some of the things that have value and worth— whether, for example, moral norms (principles, rules, virtues, etc.) about how we should treat others are *objectively true* or merely *subjectively true*. Are there moral facts just as there are biological facts and historical facts? Or is value always created by a valuer, that is, is Van Morrison's amazing body of rock 'n' soul, rhythm and blues and jazz valuable because I and many other fans value it? How much, if at all, does the goodness of X or Y depend upon the subject, depend upon whether I love X or whether it is one of my ground projects? Is it, in fact, the case that many or most good things are good *because* the subject, because you or I, love them or value them in some way? Or are good or bad, right or wrong, in many cases simply a matter of the way reality is—what just is the case with things? Is reality shot through with value and truth? Or do we humans bring value and truth to the real world by what we love and what we believe? In short, do we *discover* value? Or is value *invented* by us?

You have probably noticed that you seem to disagree with many Americans about some basic moral issues such as capital punishment, abortion, premarital or extramarital sex, immigration, cheating, and lying. And educated people are aware of just how much variety there is in the world when it comes to morality and other goods like beauty and truth. You've probably read stories from anthropologists about tribes in Africa where polygamy is (or has been) the norm, or about the old practice of some Native American tribes of killing elderly parents. Perhaps you're aware of comparatively permissive attitudes toward nudity and sex in Europe, particularly in Scandinavian countries. In short, you're probably impressed with how different people seem to be when it comes to morality and how to treat others.

We could tell similar stories about attitudes and practices related to other values of beauty, religion, and truth. No matter what I am teaching, the one thing I know I can expect my students to say is something like, "Even though everybody has a different view on this . . . ," the conviction being that the one thing we can agree on, the one thing every educated person knows, is that when it comes to beliefs about what is right and wrong, good and bad, we all have our own "different" views. So even within our own country, moral differences and disagreements are taken for granted. When it comes to questions of living well, it seems to many of us that there are almost as many different views as there are people.

In the face of this apparent diversity it is easy for us to conclude "different strokes for different folks" and to think that moral differences are more or less like differences in *taste*. Some people like fried okra and sweet ice tea; other people don't. (Go figure!) Some people like ketchup (or catsup, for that matter), others don't. And, similarly, some people think that it is wrong to cheat on a spouse or to view pornography; other people don't. Everyone, we may be inclined to say, is different. So, it's easy for us to conclude that when it comes to living well, to what we should value, to which ground projects we should commit ourselves, the answer is essentially *subjective*. This is to say that any and all norms that should guide us are the product of some individual *subject*—of you or I or the person down the street or across the river—or some individual *subjects*—some group of people such as my family, your club, their country.[2] To believe that morality and living

2. I am here conflating *subjectivism*, which philosophers typically take to be a theory

well is *subjective* is to believe that how we should treat others and what we should value is invented, not discovered, that what is worthy of our love, what is right or wrong, good or bad, beautiful or ugly, is made so by what some subject (or some coherent group of subjects) does, by what someone or some group of people believe, wish, or act upon.

> Value subjectivism, then, is the view that any and all truths about values and living well are created or invented by some particular individual(s) or subject(s) and that what is beautiful or ugly, right or wrong, good or bad, virtuous or vicious, worthy or unworthy is made so only by the feelings, attitudes, actions, cares, or beliefs of some subject or subjects, an individual or a group.

For example, if you believe that morality is subjective, then you think the normal way to proceed in thinking about morality is to somehow figure out what is right and wrong for yourself and to let others figure out what is right and wrong for themselves because morality is always and only, at bottom, about ourselves, about what we as particular individuals think or feel. You will not be too surprised if your moral answers differ from others, for there is no moral truth to be discovered, or at least no moral truth about anything other than what you or some other persons or groups feel or want or believe. You are each making your own kind of music, creating your own particular kind of morality. Why think that what is right for you will be found to be right by someone who is not you, someone who is much differ-ent from you? You've probably heard people say, "I know abortion is wrong for me, that I could never have an abortion, but I can't say it would be wrong for someone else," and "Although I could never do X"—replace X with the sexual activity of your choice—"who's to say it is wrong for someone else to do X?" And you probably deal with vegetarianism and veganism this same way—we are not morally required not to eat meat, you think; vegetarian-ism or veganism is required only if you believe it or want it to be morally required.

Value subjectivism, whether the values be moral, aesthetic, political, religious, etc., understands matters of value as being most similar to matters

---

about how individuals are related to moral norms, with what is typically referred to as *cultural relativism*, which I take to be a subset of *group subjectivism*. *Cultural relativism* maintains that morality is the product not of individuals but of some particular group of individuals and/or their way of life. What these positions have in common is their denial that any moral truths exist that were not created or invented by some person or some group of persons.

of taste, for which there is no accounting.[3] Some people actually don't like Brussels sprouts, even roasted Brussels sprouts! Others do. I've known people to enjoy putting peanut butter on pickles or potato chips. (Okay, I made that up—but I imagine there are such people.) Perhaps, like me, you can hardly bear to think about such things. Still, we might think of such tastes as odd, or more politely, as unusual, but we would not consider such tastes mistaken or wrong, for many of us don't think there is a truth of the matter when it comes to whether or not roasted Brussels sprouts or cilantro tastes good. According to the value subjectivist, this is how we ought to think about all values. It is not that some views are true and others are mistaken. It is not that there is any more of a "truth of the matter" for morality and living well than for the fittingness of peanut butter on pickles. People are just different when it comes to tastes, and different is good.[4] And so it is with the good life and how we should live, who we should be and what we should do. My opposition to lying is, the subjectivist argument goes, like my opposition to okra (unless it is fried, in which case my opposition dissipates)—a matter purely of individual preference, of taste. And, although tastes may vary, there are no standards to which we can appeal to show that one taste is superior to others.

Indeed, one might even appeal to the Bible to support some sort of value subjectivism. There are many actions that seem to be approved of by God's people in Old Testament times (to put it quite imprecisely) that we now think are wrong—for example, polygamy, the stoning of "sinners," and animal sacrifice. Sometimes even some New Testament authors seem to endorse value subjectivism. St. Paul seems to think that whether or not it is wrong to eat meat that has been offered to idols is a matter for the individual to determine. It may be permissible for some, but not for others (1 Cor 10:23–30). A little earlier (1 Cor 7:8–9), Paul seems to suggest that whether or not it is good to marry is subject to the individual's beliefs or needs. If you want to marry, fine. If not, that's fine too.

It is important not to confuse and conflate value subjectivism with an attitude or posture of *value tolerance*. The *tolerant* person may find another person's behavior troublesome, may believe that the other person ought not to be doing some action and ought to know he ought not to be doing that action or feeling that emotion. For example, he shouldn't be dropping f-bombs

3. I am assuming here that that one who is a moral subjectivist is likely also to be a value subjectivist. That needn't be the case; one could be a moral subjectivist but not an aesthetic subjectivist, and vice versa. Still, for our purposes it does no harm to paint with broad strokes here.

4. You might puzzle a moment over what a value subjectivist could mean when she says, "Different is good."

in public conversation. But, as a *tolerant* person, she does not interfere when he drops an f-bomb, does not coerce him to do the right, or better, thing or reprimand him for his unworthy and inappropriate language. The *tolerant* person may think it wrong for Sam to consume so much, may think it harms Sam's soul for her to care so much about material possessions, but she will not interfere with her moneymaking and spending activities.[5] She tolerates Sam's troublesome actions and emotions. The *value subjectivist*, unlike the tolerant person, believes there is no truth of the matter, as such, about the wrongness or badness of hyper-consumption. Whether it is good or right for Sam to spend her time in some particular way is for Sam (or some group to which she belongs) to determine. In other words, if value subjectivism is true, then tolerance will be virtuous only for those individuals who make it to be so.[6]

There may be some good reasons to find value subjectivism an attractive, if not a compelling, picture of morality. It seems to fit some Scripture and it fits rather well with much of our experience. How could I possibly know whether or not it is appropriate for you to put a tattoo (a cross, no doubt) on your left buttock, and not where everybody can see it? Isn't that between you and God? How dare anyone tell your grandfather how he has to die? He's got to make that decision, before God. And surely the choice of a vocation—your decision to pursue elementary or middle school teaching rather than engineering—is a moral matter, but we don't think someone else should tell us which vocation is the right or wrong one for us.[7]

5. Insofar as her not interfering is expressive of her *tolerance*, then not just any reason explains why she does not interfere. For example, one might not interfere with Sam's spending habits because Sam is rather strong, has a short fuse, and does not appreciate being corrected or interfered with. In that case, noninterference is more expressive of the virtue of prudence.

6. Of course, the moral subjectivist will owe us an account of exactly how individuals or groups may make an action or a virtue morally required.

7. We need to keep clear the distinction between, on the one hand, the individual having to make a decision for herself and, on the other hand, the individual's decision, whatever it is, being right precisely *because* the individual herself has made the decision. It is trivially true that in value matters we have to decide for ourselves. How is it even possible for anyone else to make a decision for us? Subjectivism in at least some of its forms holds both that in some sense *our deciding something* makes it right, as well as that the individual must decide for herself. Non-subjectivists admit only that to be an agent is to make decisions for oneself.

5.1.2 God, Goods, and Value: Some Problems of Value Subjectivism

Despite how attractive, at first glance, value subjectivism may appear, one implication of the core Christian experience and Christian identity is that value subjectivism is, at best, a confused and incomplete picture, that it doesn't adequately track the way we know the world to be. Here's why. Let's assume that value subjectivism is true. If so, then when I consider the world's hungry children and think, "That's not the way things are supposed to be," I am either expressing a feeling I have (i.e., I disapprove or feel sad about there being hungry children) or I am stating something that I believe to be true, but true only for this subject—me—or the particular group to which I belong, my club, or my church, or my school, or my country. There's no truth of the matter independent of me for me or anyone else to discover. I'm not really claiming that there are duties about feeding hungry children that anyone could and should know, I'm merely stating my beliefs (or expressing my feelings) much as if I were to say, "You shouldn't fry pickles in butter."

I, by contrast, believe that the presence of hungry children is not compatible with the shalom God desires for God's creation. What you or I want does not change this fact. The world should have no hungry children. If, when Randy considers the world's hungry children, he thinks not about how tragic it is that children go hungry—perhaps the well-being of children does not register with him at all—but only the feeling "I'm glad that the world is constructed in such a way that *I* am not hungry," then in at least that one respect things in the world *are* the way they are supposed to be, as far as Randy is concerned. He is not hungry, and that is primarily what he cares about.

And if value subjectivism is true, Randy and I are not really disagreeing about whether there should be hungry children. According to the value subjectivist, even my judgment about the evil of children in hunger and what you and I owe to hungry children is not really a judgment about the way the world is, but a statement or expression about myself and what I believe or feel; it is a statement about me. According to value subjectivism, whenever you or I make a value statement, we are each really just stating our own value feelings or convictions—truths about ourselves and our desires or emotions, not about the world external to us. There is, according to value subjectivism, no "way things are supposed to be," only ways that you or I would like them to be or think they should be. And if we happen to differ, well, we happen to differ, much as we may differ about how much better than a chocolate donut a hot Krispy Kreme donut is. (Infinitely better, if you ask me.) But, is that what we really think? Do you and I really think that the goodness or badness in the world is in how we feel or what we think, a matter of our own interests, whatever these may be?

In *Rumors of Another World*, Philip Yancey reports these chilling words of Heinrich Himmler, head of the SS during the Nazi reign in Germany:

> What happens to the Russians, what happens to the Czechs, is a matter of utter indifference to me. . . . Whether the other nationalities live in comfort or perish of hunger interests me only insofar as we need them as slaves for our society; apart from that, it does not interest me. Whether or not 10,000 Russian women collapse from exhaustion while digging a tank ditch interests me only insofar as it affects the completion of the tank ditch for Germany.[8]

If value subjectivism is true, if right and wrong, good and bad, beautiful and ugly, always refer back to the moral agent (or her group) and *only* the moral agent (or her group), what is our appropriate response to Himmler's words?

Well, we can say that our moral views are different from his, much as we might say to someone who puts ketchup in his coffee that our tastes differ from his. But most of us would not say only this. Most of us, thank God, would say that we are glad there are few people who share Himmler's moral views, that we are appalled at Himmler's failure to grasp the value of human life, and that he failed to recognize that *every* human life has value. If value subjectivism is true, what we cannot say to Himmler and his ilk is that their views are mistaken or false or inferior in some way to our very different values; we cannot say that their views fail to track moral reality. We cannot say what most of us cannot help believing very deeply: that human lives matter, and matter equally, and not just because you and I want them to. For, according to value subjectivism, there is no value reality external to moral agents; there is no way things are meant to be, morally speaking. Himmler's contempt for the well-being of 10,000 Russian women is not morally wrong, just different.

Could this possibly be true? Could Himmler's view possibly be only different, but no worse than our contrasting view of the value of the lives of those ten thousand Russian women? Few of us think this could be the way things really are. Persons *do* matter; lives do matter. Christians are not alone in believing that the lives of those ten thousand Russian women mattered. They mattered to God, whether or not they mattered to Himmler, and they should matter to us. We think Himmler is mistaken, and morally wrong, not to believe that they matter, not to care about them. So, value subjectivism

8. Yancey, *Rumors of Another World*, 117.

does not square well with our strong intuitions and our common moral convictions that others, like Himmler, can be wrong in what they care about.

Nor does value subjectivism square well with the conviction that we ourselves can be mistaken about values. If you look at yourself and notice that you are constantly tempted to lie in order to save yourself from hurt or harm, you may bemoan your character: "I wish I were a better person, less tempted to lie." By contrast, I may notice my own tendency to tell lies and think, "I am such a good person, knowing how to protect myself." According to value subjectivism, what it is to be a good person and whether we hit or miss that mark is determined *only* by me or you or our respective groups—there is no truth of the matter as such about being a good person. Right and wrong, good and bad, are a matter of invention or self-authorship, not a matter of discovery. So, there is a problem with feeling tempted to lie only if I think or feel that there is a problem. But can this really be so? Couldn't you aspire to be the sort of person it would not be right or good for you to be? Haven't we all had such aspirations, at times? Isn't the self-satisfied racist vile, although he takes pride in his racism? Definitely. So what sort of person we ought to be is not merely a matter of what we or some other group believe or feel. There's a truth of the matter about who and what we ought to be that we don't invent.

So far, in thinking about value subjectivism we've appealed only to our common intuitions, common beliefs about right and wrong, good and bad. Our argument has been, "If value subjectivism is true, then here's what the world must really be like. But, think about that. Consult your intuitions, your deep sense of how the world really is. Is the world really the way the value subjectivist thinks it is? Most of us—and not only Christians—don't think so." Of course, this is not an argument that would persuade all value subjectivists. A subjectivist might respond, for example, "Perhaps your intuitions are mistaken. Believing something to be so doesn't make it so."[9] Still, most of us find our intuitions about morality and other values much more palatable than value subjectivism. We think our beliefs that reality isn't really the way the value subjectivist takes it to be are warranted, are appropriately so unshakeable that they count strongly against value subjectivism, even if we don't have a proof for these deep beliefs.

Another thing to note is that to this point in our consideration of value subjectivism we've made no appeal to belief in God or to any other Christian belief. We've assumed that most thoughtful and reflective folk have intuitions that aren't easily squared with value subjectivism so that

---

9. J. L. Mackie is an example of a philosopher who thinks that our common moral views do, indeed, assume an objective moral reality and that these common moral views are false. See his *Ethics*.

most reflective folk—Christians and other theists, polytheists, agnostics, and atheists—have some initial reasons to be suspicious of value subjectivism. Are there particularly Christian reasons that might count against the plausibility of value subjectivism?

Consider, how does the value subjectivist's view of morality fit with our experience of God? How does it fit with the psalmist's plea, "Search me, O God, and know my heart; test me and know my thoughts. See if there is any wicked way in me . . ." (Ps 139:23–24)? Or David's confession that he has done evil and that God's judgment upon him is justified?

Not well, I think. In both cases the assumption is that when it comes to one's goodness before God there *is* a truth of the matter, a truth God knows far better than the individual herself knows it. What sense would the words of the psalmist here make if value subjectivism were true? If value subjectivism were the whole story, then in knowing your "wicked ways" God would know only whether you measure up to your own standards, whatever they are, not whether you measure up to some standards of goodness that existed before you were born and will exist after you die. (Indeed, if value subjectivism were the case, some training in positive thinking skills might considerably improve the world. Aim lower, and commend yourself for aiming lower, and you will more likely achieve your goal. And achieving your goals is a good thing—well, at least most of us think it is.) But if this were sufficient, if all we really need is more robust egos and more positive self-assessments, what sense would God's forgiveness of our sins make? Why would God need to re-create this world through Jesus Christ if things are not really broken, but we just look at them as though they are? Indeed, God's redemptive activity would look rather silly, an over-the-top action if ever there were one.

5.1.3. God, Goods, and Value: Value Objectivism

God became incarnate in Jesus Christ and lived and died as a human and rose again from the dead because things are not the way they are supposed to be. Christ came down in order to restore things to their good estate precisely because there is something really wrong with us and with the world in which we live, because it is true that things aren't the way they are supposed to be and God knows it. The shalom that is good, that God desires for us, has been destroyed. That shalom is good and that shalom has been destroyed by human actions is a discovery we make, not a "truth" we may or may not choose to invent. Things aren't bad in the world just because we feel things are bad. Things really are bad; things really aren't the way they are supposed to be, and your or my thinking the contrary doesn't change that fact.

No, Christians have good reason to believe that there really is something wrong with a world in which children starve to death, in which innocent babies and children are separated from their parents, in which children are pressed into war, in which husbands and boyfriends hit women, in which people are hated merely because of the color of their skin, in which the weak and feeble are left to fend for themselves, in which we destroy the world we live in just because we want more things. All these things are wrong, and no one's believing otherwise can make them right and good. Likewise, no matter what we may think about ourselves, Christians believe that we all have fallen short of what God would have us be; we don't love as we should love. We can't change our condition as sinners merely by believing that we are not sinful.

Christian experience and self-understanding thus entails that there are truths about our moral condition, truths that are not created by us and that may even be unknown to us. (Perhaps we don't believe them because we don't want to believe them.) God, however, knows the truth about our moral condition, and because God knows the truth and is full of sorrow over this truth, God embarks upon a project of redemption to restore us to what God desires for us, to create a new heaven and a new earth. At the very least, then, Christian experience implies that any complete map of values and living well must include a significant area of *value objectivism*.[10] To endorse *value objectivism* is to believe that at least some value norms, truths about what is worthy of our love and what we should and should not be and do, exist independently of what any human subject[11] may think or do with respect to moral norms. Whether or not lying is wrong is not determined by what some subject or subjects believe or do; honesty is not a virtue merely because I, or my culture, affirm it to be so. If I needlessly harm an innocent person, then no matter what any person or group believes, I have done wrong. To meaningfully say that I have sinned against God and do not deserve God's grace is to say that there is a truth of the matter that exists independently of any person's beliefs about sin, a truth known by God and knowable by me.

10. The value objectivism I describe here is a robust form, but not the only possible form, of what contemporary philosophers term *moral (value) realism*.

11. Here I leave open the important and vexed question of whether one should be a *divine value subjectivist*, believing that all or much value, right and wrong, good and evil, etc., are the products of some divine thought, feeling, or action, rather than a thought, feeling, or action of an individual human subject or a group of human subjects. See the following section for a little more on this problem.

Value objectivism holds that at least some truths about values—moral values as well as other types of values—are discovered by us, not invented, that some value truths exist independently of the beliefs, attitudes, and feelings of particular humans or groups of humans.

5.2 GOD, CREATION, AND THE COMPLEXITY OF VALUES

To say that Christians ought to be value objectivists of some sort is not to make the additional (and fairly preposterous) claim that a comprehensive picture of values, and of morality, in particular, can be an exclusively *objectivist* one, and to claim that there is no room at all for subjectivism in a complete picture. For example, we have good reason to think that some moral norms *are* morally subjective. My own view—one that I'll just assert and not argue for at this point—is that vegetarianism may fall into this category. I myself think that, given the current practices of the food industry, and especially given the impact of our consumption of beef upon global climate change, there are good moral reasons to eat lower on the food chain (and not only moral but economic and prudential reasons as well), but I'm not sure that it is always morally wrong for me and for others to eat meat. Instead, I suspect that we are morally required to eat a lot less meat than Americans typically do. On the other hand, I don't think Elizabeth's conscience is necessarily mistaken in her conviction that she ought not to eat meat. What makes it permissible for me occasionally to eat meat, but not for Elizabeth to eat meat, are our respective convictions on the matter of eating meat. Likewise, my decision to pursue a career in basketball or rock 'n' roll may be right for me even though it means that I cannot become the master cellist that you have chosen to be.

We can also accommodate a fair amount of subjectivism at the cultural level. There are styles of dress appropriate for some American Christians that would be inappropriate for some African Christians, and vice versa. And in a poor country with a long history of bribery as a cultural practice, it may be morally permissible to bribe police officers and other officials, although it would not be permissible (or prudent!) for you or me to try this in Minnesota. Some argue—and this, perhaps surprisingly, is a vexing question—that in certain cultural contexts Christians should be permitted to have more than one spouse. To embrace moral objectivism is not to claim that *all* moral truths are objective and universal; it is not to claim that there are no particular or subjective truths about how we ought to live. It is, rather, to claim that *some* truths about morality and, perhaps, other values exist independently of how individuals believe or feel about them, much as the truth *North Carolina is south of South Dakota* is true regardless of what folks may think or feel about it.

A not insignificant difficulty, but a difficulty we needn't resolve right now, is determining *which* norms are objective and which are subjective, is determining when we should be content to let a matter rest with an individual conscience or a cultural "conscience" and when we should make every effort to ensure that consciences conform to the good that can be discovered and known. The cultural push in our current age here in the developed Western world will dispose us to contract the realm of value objectivity and to expand the realm of subjective value, especially subjective morality, although historically that has not always been the case. At any rate, we do well to resist this tendency to expand the realm of the subjective while reducing the realm of the objective, lest what Christians believe to be objectively wrong actions are reinterpreted merely as matters of personal taste—lest we tolerate more, and more profound, evil than should be tolerated.

The creation accounts of Genesis remind us that God's creation was originally good. In one account, God sees Adam alone and says, "It is not good that the man should be alone; I will make him a helper as his partner" (Gen 2:18). The serpent tempts Eve by promising her knowledge of good and evil (Gen 3:5). Thus, this is a world in which good and bad, right and wrong, may be discovered, and are not invented by the convictions or feelings of Adam and Eve, of some moral agent. The Christian Scriptures remind us that there is a way things are meant to be and enable us to see that things now are no longer the way that God meant them to be, that the world has become a place straying from and in rebellion against the goodness God desires for God's creation.

The world God created is beautiful and good and wonderfully rich and complex. And there is a moral cast to this reality—the way things ought to be, the way things are when things are going along with God's intentions for things. That is how God created the universe. You and I do not bring morality to the way things are; it's already there. We either do our best to align ourselves with the moral bent of God's created order or we work at cross-purposes with it. Unfortunately, as Christians know, too often our beliefs and our feelings about right and wrong, good and bad, are as mistaken as our actions.

Martin Luther King Jr. (1929–68)

In 1954 Martin Luther King Jr. received a call to be the pastor of the Dexter Avenue Baptist Church in Montgomery, Alabama. That same year in *Brown v. Board of Education* the United States Supreme Court had declared that racial segregation in public schools was unconstitutional. King's work as a pastor—and King always understood himself to be, first and foremost, a pastor—meant taking seriously the suffering and the oppression of his congregation. By late 1955 that meant for King taking a leadership role in the civil rights movement, the struggle of blacks for freedom and equality in the United States. As he said to those gathered at a meeting of the Montgomery Improvement Association in December 1955, "There comes a time when people get tired of being trampled over by the iron feet of oppression."

Often in the 1950s and early 1960s the iron feet of oppression were shod in slippers or cushioned shoes. That is to say that most of the white folks in the South (most of whom considered themselves Christian) and probably most of the white folks in the entire nation (most of whom considered themselves religious, if not Christian) didn't recognize their own iron feet. Most folks believed that it was right to treat black people differently because they believed black people were inferior. Most folks believed they weren't doing anything wrong by telling Rosa Parks and other blacks to go sit at the back of the bus, or to eat and drink in their own separate places. Most folks believed that blacks deserved different—and even unequal—treatment.

But Martin Luther King Jr. and the civil rights movement would have none of it. They organized. They marched. They marched peacefully as police with dogs attacked them, as they were sprayed by water cannons, as they were beaten with clubs. They marched peacefully. At the conclusion of the historic march from Selma to Montgomery, Martin spoke to the people: "I know you are asking today, 'How long will it take? . . . How long will prejudice blind the visions of men, darken their understanding, and drive bright-eyed wisdom from her sacred throne? . . . How long will justice be crucified and truth bear it?' I come to say to you this afternoon, however difficult the moment, however frustrating the hour, it will not be long, because 'truth crushed to earth will rise again.' How long? Not long, because 'no lie can live forever.' How long? Not long, because the arc of the moral universe is long, but it bends towards justice."[12] King believed that we live in a moral universe,

---

12. King, "Address at the Conclusion of the Selma to Montgomery March."

a universe in which we can discover right and wrong, good and evil, and choose to do the good and the right. King believed that there is justice and injustice and that these are part of the nature of things, not a matter of what some persons or group of persons believe, for as King knew so well, it isn't hard to find people who fail to recognize and do what true justice requires.

In his 1963 "Letter from a Birmingham Jail" to a group of Alabama clergy, a letter King wrote as he was in jail for nonviolent civil disobedience, King wrote, "Any law that uplifts human personality is just. Any law that degrades human personality is unjust."[13] Certain ways of treating human beings are wrong, even if people think they are right. Degrading human beings is wrong, morally impermissible. That is a truth of the moral universe in which we live. If people believe that all people are not moral equals entitled to respect, they are mistaken. If laws that dishonor and demean others are enacted, they are not genuine laws, and they should be disobeyed.

King never wavered in his commitment to living, and encouraging others to live, aligned with a universe that bends toward justice. He showed us that we can do better, and because of his leadership Americans have done better than we might otherwise have done. But there is often a price to be paid for doing justice, loving mercy, and walking humbly with God, and encouraging others to do the same. Martin Luther King Jr. was assassinated in Memphis, Tennessee, on April 4, 1968, but his dream and his hope for the moral bent of the universe lives on.

Put Down the Phone: For Further Thought

1. What facts do you know that lead you to think that value subjectivism of some sort might be true? Can you identify some specific areas of life in which subjectivism rings truer than in others? Can you think of areas of life in which subjectivism fails to ring true?

2. Can you think of good nonreligious reasons not to be a value subjectivist? That is, might someone who is not a Christian or a theist still have good reasons not to be a value subjectivist?

3. Do you think moral values are enough like other values so that the term "value objectivism" makes sense? Or do we need to discuss the different types of values individually? For example, does it make more

13. King, "Letter from a Birmingham Jail," 430.

sense to be a moral objectivist than to be an aesthetic objectivist? Why or why not?

4. Are there things that you think a morally decent person can't help knowing are good or bad, wrong or right? Does everyone have some knowledge of objective morality? How could we explain this?

5. How do you explain cultural practices—for example, female circumcision/genital mutilation—that seem to you obviously a violation of objective morality, given the harm they do? If such cultural practices are violations of objective morality, why doesn't every culture recognize this? Can you think of any practices within your culture that others might recognize as violations of objective morality?

6. A cornerstone of Dr. Martin Luther King Jr.'s civil rights work was his belief in the dignity of all human beings and his conviction that certain things are right and wrong independent of whether we believe them to be right and wrong, beliefs that were based on his beliefs about God and God's story. Could one/should one have as strong a commitment to protecting the dignity of all human beings without a belief in God? How? Why?

6

FROM CHRIST TO THE WORLD
God's Character and God's Project

In the last chapter I argued that Christians, and not only Christians but also those who may have no religious belief at all, have good reason to believe that there are truths about values, including moral values, and that some or many of these truths are independent of us. Many of our actions and emotions share in these values and have sometimes more, sometimes less of whatever values they possess. Consider my very elementary West Coast Swing dance. Arguably, my dance has some aesthetic value, but it is neither beautiful nor agile. It lacks significant aesthetic value (in contrast, if I do say so myself, to my basketball hook shot). My dance may also possess some economic value if I am competing in a dance competition with a cash prize. And it has moral or ethical value as well. One can swing one's partner recklessly, and in a manner that may do harm not only to the partner but to others on the dance floor or in the audience. I argued that, in many cases, the value that our actions and emotions may possess or lack is independent of your or my particular beliefs or feelings about the action or emotion. My thinking that my swing dance is safe or smooth doesn't make it so. Certain things—for example, kindness to an immigrant, sharing a meal with a friend, or a Scriabin piano sonata—have value whether or not you or I recognize them as valuable. Theists, believers in a perfect God who created the universe, appropriately believe that there are moral truths, aesthetic truths, religious truths, and so on, and that God knows these truths. As a perfect being, God acts in accordance with this knowledge—a perfect being could not intend an action that being knew would harm a person unnecessarily.

You and I may also know many of these truths and we may act or fail to act in ways that comport with what we know. I may be morally required to give more than 10 percent of my net income to the poor even if I don't think I'm morally required to do so; I may not value what I ought to value. You and I don't *invent* moral value—at least not all of what is morally valuable—we *discover* it. It is part of the fabric of the world we inhabit. And the same is true of many other types of value. Some people are worthy not only of our respect but also of our admiration and appreciation. Some objects— buildings and visual artworks, dances, piano sonatas, sunsets, birdsongs, etc.—are worthy of our appreciation, even if something prevents us from actually feeling admiration or appreciation. Christians profess that God is the creator of everything that exists that is created.[1] Christians believe that God has created a world in which what is true about beauty and goodness and rightness and human flourishing is not simply a matter of what you or I or some group to which we belong believes or somehow determines to be true. As I argued in the last chapter, because God exists, the world is value-laden, shot through with value, and much of that character of things exists independently of you and me.

A cornerstone of Christianity as we've described it, after all, is that we humans have done some things and we continue to do things that are wrong or bad and that harm God's creation and disrupt a good relationship with God and the creation. We turn our back upon the good and loving God and, instead, turn toward our desires and apparent interests. In doing so, we often hurt ourselves, hurt others, and hurt God and our relationship with God. We can't make our abuse of God's creation and our ignoring the needs of those who are weak and vulnerable okay or morally permissible just by thinking they are okay or by not valuing those things, because the truth is that they are not okay. They are wrong, they are evil. Ignoring the needs of the weak and those who are vulnerable harms individuals created in the image of God. The universe created by God is ineluctably moral. There is, Christians believe, a way that things are meant to be. As Dr. Martin Luther King Jr. said, "The arc of the moral universe is long but it bends towards

---

1. We need to make this qualification: God is the creator of all *created* things, but not all things, because God pretty clearly is not the creator of everything. For example, God exists, but God did not create God. Are there possibly other things that exist that God did not create? You might wonder whether God is the creator of every truth; did God have to do anything, create anything, to make the proposition "*God exists*" true? Or that *God is a perfect being*?

justice." That's the kind of universe a good and loving Creator has made. That's the kind of world we live in.

In this chapter we'll consider a second implication of basic Christian experience and understanding of God. We'll try to see what follows from our beliefs about God's identity, that is to say, God's nature and character, for what we should value and how we should live. If God is the person Christians believe God is, what does that mean for our loving the good and trying to live a good life?

6.1 THE CHARACTER OF GOD

Thesis 2: Christians have encountered a God who knows and loves goodness, a God who has created our world for the good of shalom, a ground project aimed at the good for all of God's creation. Christians encounter a God of faithful and steadfast love for us and the creation. Christians have met a God who is ever ready to bless us and to forgive our wrongs as God works to achieve God's project of shalom.

Some philosophical problems may be interesting and important philosophically, yet practically irrelevant to the life of the Christian in light of her experience with God (the last footnote above being a case in point). Some reflective individuals will, and should, ponder these abstract philosophical and theological questions even if they have no bearing upon how to live faithfully to one's Creator. Knowing the truth may matter, simply because the truth is about God or the world created by God, even if knowledge of some particular truth may have no apparent impact upon how one lives. One might wonder, for example, just exactly how the objective moral reality described in the previous chapter is related to God even if the answer to that question will have no impact upon what one chooses. Did God create moral reality in the same way that God created humans as bipeds rather than tripeds? That is, could God have created a different moral reality in the same way that God could have created a much different sort of human? Could God create a universe in which a crushed human head is beautiful? Or were God's choices in creating the universe constrained in some way—perhaps by something in God's nature, perhaps by the necessary character of the way reality is?

One famous example of philosophical wrestling with this problem occurs in Plato's *Euthyphro*. Euthyphro, a person recognized in Athens for his religious character and wisdom, has decided to prosecute his father for murder. His father had bound a slave accused of wrongdoing and left him in a ditch, abandoned to the elements, while they waited for the proper authorities. The slave died from exposure. Euthyphro believes his father is culpable for the slave's death. Had his father taken care, the slave would still be alive. His father's actions brought about the death of the slave, so Euthyphro is pressing charges against him.

In ancient Athens it was unheard of to prosecute one's father, yet Euthyphro insists that it is the right thing to do. Socrates puzzles with Euthyphro over this question. Why does Euthyphro think it right? What could possibly make it right to prosecute one's father? One answer, of course, is that something is right to do because God (or, in the ancient Greece of the *Euthyphro*, the gods) requires it. Of course, the deeper question is this: what is the relation between God and goodness or between God and what is right? If God requires us to do something, why does God require this? *Is an action right merely because God requires it? Or does God require some action because it is right and God knows it to be right?* Does God *create* moral reality or does God know moral reality and create a world in light of the moral truth God knows?[2]

The attempt to better understand the relation between God and goodness is important for theologians and philosophers alike. But as the story of Abraham and Isaac (Gen 22:1–19) makes clear, it may not be practically relevant; it may make no practical difference to how Christians should live. When God commands Abraham to sacrifice Isaac, Abraham's son, a son through whom God has promised to bless not only Abraham but all nations, Abraham is puzzled. How can God bless the nations through him if he obeys God and kills Isaac, and Isaac is dead? Mustn't the potential for blessing through Isaac end with his death? Abraham does not puzzle over whether God has commanded this sacrifice of Isaac *because it is right* or whether it is right *because God commanded it*, or even whether it could be right for God to command this. Abraham's struggle, instead, is a matter of how he will respond to the only true God, this God he knows to be faithful and loving, this God he loves, when this God requires him to sacrifice his

---

2. If we were speaking of the human relation to goodness we would ask whether we *invent* moral goodness or whether we *discover* it. But that doesn't quite work with God, does it? Even if God does not invent moral goodness, as a perfect, all-knowing, and everlasting being, it isn't the case that at some particular time God acquires moral knowledge that God had previously lacked. A perfect, everlasting, all-knowing being at no time lacks knowledge, so it isn't that God *discovers* moral truths. Rather, if God does not invent moral truths, then it seems most plausible that God, being God, has always known these moral truths, that as an everlasting all-knowing being, God does not discover truth but everlastingly knows what is true.

beloved son, Isaac. How can he love well when love conflicts with love?[3] How can he love God, who has commanded him to kill Isaac, and, obeying God, nevertheless love Isaac?

Most Christians, even while granting the legitimacy of Socrates's concern, likely will identify more with Abraham and his struggle than with the philosopher who is trying to understand how God may be related to goodness or morality. The core Christian experience, as we've seen, is an encounter with God and a response to God. We meet a God who is our Creator, who wants to be in fellowship with us and invites us to that fellowship. We discover, however, that the world has turned from God and that we are more inclined to follow the world than God, despite the goodness of the creation and God's goodness to us. Because of our wrong loving and our wrongdoing, because of our failure to love God, to love all those who bear God's image, and to love in a fitting and appropriate way all that God has created, we are not in proper relation to God; nor are we related properly to other persons and to God's creation. In this encounter with God, then, we become aware of our alienation from God, from our neighbors, from the created order, and even from ourselves. We see how much we and our world need healing. We discover, in short, that things are not the way God wants them to be, things are not the way they are supposed to be.

Nevertheless, as we have seen, in our encounter with God we meet One who is resolved to make right what has gone wrong with things. The God we meet is committed to healing and repairing the creation, a God with a ground project of making all things new who is willing to pay the greatest of costs in order to heal and make right a disordered people and a disordered creation. In their encounter with God, Christians discover a steadfast, unfailing love and God's readiness always to forgive and to make things right. In knowing the Jesus who lived, suffered, died, and was raised from the dead by God, we know a God of love, a God always *for* us. We may not love this God as we should. We may even sometimes doubt God's existence or God's concern for us. But there is no other God in whom we can believe or to whom we can turn. The God encountered by Christians is a good God, a God of love who, because God loves, acts in history and in our lives to bring about God's own good purposes for the creation, a God who works to establish God's ground project of *shalom*.

Christians have a general picture of how God wants things to turn out, a general picture of what is the point of our existence and of all that has been created. The Westminster Catechism (1642–47), a centuries-old

3. Søren Kierkegaard's discussion of Abraham and Isaac in his pseudonymously authored *Fear and Trembling* is a masterpiece of insight into Abraham's struggle.

collection of questions and answers intended to summarize the basics of Christian faith, opens with the question, "What is our chief end, the *telos* or the point, of our lives?" and answers that our goal, the point of our being, is "to glorify and enjoy God forever." God is glorified and enjoyed well and fittingly when humans are in right relationship with God, with one another and themselves, and with all that God has created. As Irenaeus, a Greek theologian of the second century, wrote, "The Glory of God is a person fully living, and for a person to live fully is to see God and love God's projects."[4] God is glorified and enjoyed best when *shalom,* God's project in creation and restoration, is realized.

The story of the world, the story of reality, is really God's story, not the human story. That might at first appear disheartening to us, for it seems to require a revision of our sense of our importance in the grand scheme of things. But precisely because the story of the universe is God's story it is also, albeit derivatively, our story, for the God Christians encounter is a God *for* us, a God who includes humans and the world we love in the story of the universe God creates and sustains. This God in Christ comes to the world, and loving and healing those to whom God has come, turns Christ's disciples back to the world to love and serve it, to adopt God's ground project of shalom as their ground project as well.

6.2 GOD'S CHARACTER AND FORGIVENESS

Much of God's activity in the world, from creation through re-creation and fulfillment, is aimed to bring about shalom so that all things can be what God means them to be, can be true to their natures and purposes as created by God. However, according to the Christian Scriptures, God's original aim for the creation was interrupted and has been prevented by human sin and the consequences of our sin. We chose, and we continue to choose, a path that parts from God's ways. God knows what we ought to be and do in order to contribute to and achieve shalom. God sees that we still tend to have other priorities and agendas and that we would rather aim at our own goals than aim at God's goals for us and the created order. We love ourselves with a love that should be directed to God. We love the world, the things created by God, with a love that is appropriate for the Creator but not for created things.

God might have abandoned us, might have given up on this project of the fellowship of all creation with and in God, but, according to the Christian Scriptures, God hasn't given up (John 3:16). That is not God's character.

4. This is a paraphrase of a line in Irenaeus, *Against Heresies,* bk. IV, ch. 20, 7.

Instead, God has undertaken to make things right, to heal the world, to complete God's loving aims for the world God has created. To that end, to the end of shalom, of reconciliation, of establishing and maintaining harmony with us and enabling us to live true to our created natures and so to live faithfully and well, God forgives us, and forgives again and again, seventy times seven, as often as forgiveness is needed (Luke 17:3–4).

A paradigmatic action of God in response to humans is thus forgiveness, and a primary virtue God possesses is *forgivingness*.[5] Forgiveness is a rather complex transaction or exchange, typically between at least two parties, a transaction aimed at reconciliation or a restoration to a state and relationship that existed prior to the doing of a wrong that has disturbed a relationship and has alienated the parties from one another. Or, if not a complete reconciliation and restoration of a relationship, at least a better relationship than the two parties experienced during the alienation created by a wrong. In our broken world, we should recognize that some wrongs can be so grave and the wounds so deep that a complete restoration and reconciliation of the wrongdoer and the person wronged may not be possible.[6] Peace and hope for a future in which every tear is dried (Rev 21:4) may be the best that we can now achieve.

As a transaction or exchange, forgiveness requires (1) a person who has been wronged, (2) a wrongdoer, that is to say, a guilty person, (3) an awareness of and recognition of the wrongdoing by the person who has been wronged, (4) an acknowledgment of the wrongdoing by the wrongdoer, (5) a concern of the wrongdoer to distance herself from her wrongdoing, (6) a recognition in the one wronged of the wrongdoer's concern to distance herself from her wrongdoing and an acceptance of the new distance of the wrongdoer from the wrong she has done, (7) with the aim and result that the grounds for friendship and fellowship between the two parties are restored; the breach created between the two by the wrong done is removed.

The virtue of *forgivingness*, as I understand it, is a stable and enduring disposition in an individual, aware of a wrong done to her or of dispositions to do her wrong. A person with this virtue is encouraging and supportive of a wrongdoer's acknowledging and distancing himself from the wrong that he has done and/or his dispositions to do wrong to her. And, having supported this distancing, the forgiving person now recognizes and accepts the distancing with the hope and the intention that the friendship and harmony

---

5. Roberts, "Forgivingness," 289–306.

6. I have in mind here the forgiveness, yet not complete reconciliation and restoration, that may occur when a victim of sexual violence forgives her attacker or when a spouse has been deeply, deeply betrayed by a partner. Forgiveness and healing can occur even though the two parties are not restored to where they were prior to the wrong.

disturbed by the wrong done and/or the dispositions to do wrong may be restored to at least the earlier state of the two people and that they can live in peace with one another, with hope for their futures.

Notice that forgiveness and the virtue of forgivingness presuppose at least some degree of moral objectivism or moral realism (*thesis one*) in order to get off the ground. Only if there is a real disposition to do wrong or if real wrong has been done can forgiveness occur. If I feel that somehow you have offended me, that you have wronged me, by your dissing the restaurant's, not my, Brussels sprouts, I may have a problem with you that you can help fix, but that fix will have nothing to do with genuine forgiveness. You may say to me, "You misheard me. I said these Brussels sprouts taste like a ship . . . that has sailed many seas, and in every port has picked up a flavor that has only enhanced their romantic earthiness," and all will be well. If the issue is that you have dissed my roasted Brussels sprouts (gently caramelized, with a hint of freshly grated parmesan cheese, and lightly drizzled with aged balsamic vinegar), and that by dissing the gift I had invested myself deeply in preparing for you, you have wronged me, perhaps we may recognize that you have wronged me. Then the transaction of forgiveness, a change in each of us and a restoration of our relationship, can get off the ground.

Perhaps I may be aware not of the actual wrongs I have done you but only that I am the sort of person who is likely to wrong you, even in ways I may not be fully aware of. Can forgiveness occur in this case? Or must I be able to point to a specific wrong I have done you and from which I can distance myself? I can't speak for everyone, but from having spoken with my wife and my children, I am well aware that I am not well aware of all the wrongs I have done to them, of all the things they could justifiably hold against me. I have a tendency to demand more of them than I expect of myself, though I can't identify all the instances in which I have done so. But I have tried and, I hope, will continue to try to distance myself from that tendency. And I have made it known to them that I regret that tendency and would like to change. That suffices for the healing of forgiveness to occur, for us to live in peace with one another with hope for our futures.

God's forgiveness of us proceeds, similarly, from the fact that human beings, by some of our actions, affections, emotions, or cares, have wronged God; we are guilty of wronging God. Or, as above, God's forgiveness of us may proceed from the fact that we know that we are disposed to wrong God, though we may not be aware of each and every wrong we do to God but only of our character, our disposition to fail to give God the love of which God is worthy. Theologians and philosophers have explained the exact nature of the wrong we do to God, or our disposition to wrong God, in a variety of ways—whether, for example, the origin of all our wrong lies in an improper love of self (i.e., whether pride is the root of all sin) or whether there are multiple sources of our failure to love God well. Christians agree, in any case, that "we have not loved God with our whole heart, and we have not loved our neighbors as ourselves." And, as the psalmist understood far better than I do, we do not know, we cannot count, the wrongs we do or have a tendency to do. "But who can detect their errors? Clear me from my hidden faults" (Ps 19:12). God is worthy of a different and better love than that which we typically offer God. The same is true of our love for our neighbors and our love for God's creation. That we are inclined to love poorly, to love unfittingly, and that we act upon our misdirected loves and so wrong others, remains the case whether or not we recognize it as a fact, whether or not we agree, contra Himmler, that there is some appropriate way in which we ought to love the created order, and our neighbors, and God. There is a truth about what we owe to God and to others, even if our actions and our character have made us blind to that truth.

We should also recognize that we can forgive someone only for the wrong she has done to us, and not the wrong she has done to someone else.[7] Were my daughter to steal Yo-Yo Ma's cello, and then repent of her theft, I can forgive her for the injury she has done to the family name, but I cannot forgive her for the wrong of stealing Yo-Yo Ma's cello—that's a wrong only he can forgive. We wrong God by our disordered actions and affections. God may not be the only person wronged, of course, but insofar as our wrongdoing frustrates God's project for creation, God is also wronged. Sometimes the harm we do is to a spouse, a sibling, or a student. Sometimes we may injure a part of the created order, as when we consume what we ought not to or consume more than we should, or when we dump toxins in rivers or destroy mountaintops. Even in these cases, we might say that although God is not *directly* wronged, God is *indirectly* wronged. In harming God's creation, we act in a way that is at cross-purposes with God's loves and God's projects in creation. The wrong we do travels through its direct object to God and God's projects, to what God is aiming to accomplish. When we do wrong, the wrong we do is thus *always* a wronging of God, though not *only* a wronging of God, and perhaps not a direct wronging of God. In sin we always directly wrong or harm or act unfittingly toward something or someone, even if not God, and at the same time indirectly we unfittingly or wrongly act toward God's purposes for God's creation. We have affections and inclinations and dispositions to wrong others and God, and we may

7. Of course, this needs to be qualified; one can imagine situations in which one could receive the authority to forgive others on behalf of a wronged party. Arguably, a son or daughter may have the moral authority to forgive a wrong done to a demented or deceased parent.

need to distance ourselves from these rather than from some specific acts of wrongdoing. The story of our wrongdoing is always part of God's story, although we may not be aware of that. So, often, we may need to seek the forgiveness of others as well as God.

In the practice of forgiveness, typically the wrongdoer first repents. To repent is to acknowledge that one has done wrong, or to regret and repent a disposition to do wrong, even a disposition to do wrongs of which one may not fully be aware. To repent of some action or disposition is to display remorse and a change of heart or mind by somehow distancing oneself from the wrong action or disposition. I acknowledge to the person I have wronged the wrong I have done—or, perhaps, that I may tend to do to her. An expression of repentance and apology will often suffice for this distancing: "I am sorry—I should not have lied to you. I wronged you." "I'm sorry, I have not loved you as I should." Sometimes verbal distancing is not sufficient, and some reparation is required: "I shouldn't have borrowed your car without your permission. I'll pay for all the bodywork and repairs your car now needs."

It may be a little harder to grasp how we can distance ourselves from dispositions, tendencies to act, to do things we ought not do. Harder, but not too hard. Most parents, I suspect, have heard a child say, "Dad [or Mom], why do you always say '@#!%' when you get behind a slow driver?" "Why do you always X?" We may not be aware that we have just done X; we may have no clue that whenever Y occurs, we have a tendency to do X. However, we can come to realize that we have certain habits, certain traits of character, certain vices or fixed tendencies to do things that we ought not to do, perhaps even things we may not realize that we have done.

How can we distance ourselves from dispositions or tendencies to wrong others and not just from wrong actions? In much the same way. If I realize that, even though I have not cheated on my partner, I am often tempted to do so, then I say to my partner, "I have not cheated on you, but I admit that I have been tempted to cheat. I wish that were not the case. I'm sorry." ("I could have loved you better. I didn't mean to be unkind.") Perhaps we will need to pray like the psalmist, "I don't even know all the wrongs I have done or all the wrongs I am disposed to do and would have done had things gone just a little differently. I wish I were not that person. Heal me. Cleanse me of my hidden faults."

Just as I can be guilty of doing wrongs to others of which I am unaware, given my poor character and my lack of moral perceptiveness, I can be wronged without knowing I've been wronged. Others may think badly of me because of a lie Martin has told about me. I may not know that these others are thinking badly of me and I may be ignorant that Martin caused their negative thoughts. I may not feel harmed by what Martin has done, but I am nevertheless wronged, for I did not deserve the lies Martin told about me, or the bad thoughts of others. Still, although I have been wronged, I can forgive Martin only if I am aware of the wrong Martin has done to me. God, to be sure, knows all of our wrongs and, as such, is always positioned to forgive. And God, Christians believe, is always eager and willing to forgive, to be reconciled with us.

Exactly what I do when I forgive you for a wrong you have done to me is a matter of some contention. Robert C. Roberts thinks that in forgiveness we overcome and extinguish our anger at someone we take to be responsible for having wronged us, or we forego altogether the anger we might feel at one who is responsible for wronging us.[8] In stage six as I describe it above, the forgiver accepts the distancing of the wrongdoer from the wrong that she has done. In many cases, as Roberts maintains, the forgiver's acceptance may be an overcoming of anger, of viewing "the offender as bad, alien, guilty, worthy of suffering, unwelcome, offensive, an enemy, etc.," and re-placing that with "a benevolent perception of the offender."[9] Frequently, the emotion that must be overcome is anger. Often, though, I think it is sadness rather than anger. I see the offender as bringing about the loss of something I hold dear—perhaps our relationship—by doing something that shows that he did not value appropriately what we had agreed, at least implicitly, to be of significant value. By his action, or by his tendency to act in certain ways, he has failed to value me and our friendship as he should. His distancing himself from what he said about me reassures me that his values are what I had taken them to be, and my sadness, my seeing myself as having lost something of significant value to me, is replaced by my recognition that the loss was either not a real loss or was only temporary.

Forgiveness, I've suggested, is a transaction between two parties, the wrongdoer or the person with the disposition to do wrong and the wronged, with the wrongdoer doing her part (by repenting and distancing herself from the wrong or her disposition to do wrong) to re-create and re-establish the grounds for friendship and fellowship she initially destroyed with her wrongdoing. The wrongdoer, having distanced herself from the wrong, in-vites the wronged one to respond generously to her acknowledgment and distancing of herself from the wrong she has done. I, the wronged person, may think the repentance insincere, or the reparation insufficient, given the greatness of the wrong done, and I may refuse to accept the apology,

8. Roberts thinks "anger" is not quite accurate but that it is "the least troublesome term" for the emotion that forgiveness typically overcomes. Roberts, "Forgivingness," 290.

9. Roberts, "Forgivingness," 293.

distancing, and reparation offered. ("If you were really sorry you would buy me a new monitor.") Alternatively, recognizing the good faith effort of the wrongdoer to reconcile and re-create the grounds for friendship and fellowship, I may accept these "gifts" and may thus distance the wrongdoer from the wrong in my own affections and actions toward the wrongdoer. I may treat the wrongdoer as though the wrong hadn't occurred, although, of course, both of us know that it did. I may work to feel toward the wrongdoer what I felt prior to the wrongdoing, or what I should feel toward anyone with whom I am at peace and in fellowship. I work to act and feel in this way because I value the good of the fellowship or friendship with another and because I know that my anger or sadness over the wrong done is no longer appropriate given the intentional distancing of the wrongdoer from the wrong done. With my forgiveness, the friendship, or some semblance of peace, good will, and hope, is restored and, perhaps, re-created with a generous and benevolent cast to it.

Forgiveness, then, is a most common, paradigmatic activity of God, a character trait of the God who is a God *for* us. We are not all God cares about, but God *always* cares about us and cares greatly about us. Still, perhaps the way I have described forgiveness here may strike some Christians as problematic insofar as I have established conditions that must be met before God can forgive us. According to my account, God *cannot* forgive anyone who does not repent and distance himself from his wrongdoing, or at least his tendency or disposition to wrong God, his character as one likely to wrong God and others. The repentance and self-distancing of the wrongdoer from the wrong done is the condition for any act of forgiveness, including God's forgiveness of our sins. It may be argued that this doesn't fit well with the God whom Christians encounter, the God we know to possess the virtue of forgivingness. This is the God who forgives us despite our reluctance to be forgiven and despite our loving God and the world wrongly, the Hound of Heaven who will not let us escape.[10] God forgives us, some insist, despite our unwillingness to admit our wrongdoing, despite our rebellion against being forgiven.

I do not think this is quite so. Even knowing us better than we know ourselves, possessing the virtue of forgivingness, God always desires to forgive us. God always acts to encourage us to distance ourselves from our wrongs and our tendency to do wrong; God incites us to repent. The Hound

---

10. The "Hound of Heaven" allusion is from Francis Thompson's late nineteenth-century poem of the same name. The poem presents God as a hound who relentlessly bounds after us, wherever we go, whatever we do. A nice discussion of the poet and poem may be found at https://www.patheos.com/catholic/hound-of-heaven-pat-mcnamara-07–10-2012.

of Heaven chases us, continually reminding us of God's mercy, God's love for us, and God's eagerness to be in fellowship with us. Oh, Love that will not let me go! God discloses to us a steadfast love and grace we may well find irresistible—God loves me even though I may have no interest in God or God's projects. Even though God loves us in spite of our failure to respond appropriately to this love, God does not, because God cannot, forgive us until we have repented of our wrong or our tendency to do wrong. God loves us no less for that.

Our repentance, to be sure, is always a response to some initiative on God's part, is always occasioned by some generous display of God's love or beauty, always made possible by God's aid and initiative. But our repentance remains a condition for God's forgiving us, and thus restoring and re-creating the grounds for fellowship and friendship with God. Our repentance remains a condition for God's forgiving us, even though Christians are rightly inclined to say that our repentance is not exclusively our own doing. God is always the first actor in the process of our repentance, bringing us to do what we would not do without God's help. It remains a mystery to us, perhaps, just how much our repentance is our own action, and how much it is God's. In any case, repentance is required of us in order for forgiveness to be transacted. God cannot make things right between us and God unless things are really wrong and unless we also really want things to be right—unless we, like God, desire that God's kingdom come and that God's ground project of shalom be realized.

The God to whom Christians respond is thus the God who woos us into repentance, woos us until we repent, and who forgives us when we repent. We know, for we have seen it in Jesus Christ, that God is *for* us and *for* creation; this is why God pursues us, ever ready to forgive, always inviting us into fellowship. To live well, to flourish as the sorts of beings we are, we must accept God's generosity and goodness, acknowledge and repent of our sin, and then, in fellowship with God, attempt to live our lives responsive to God's redemptive and restorative activity. To live well is to live in fellowship with God and our neighbors and God's creation, to live our lives as the sorts of creatures we are meant to be. To live well is to live with hope for the day when God's project of shalom will be accomplished, to live faithfully in the time in which the beginning of God's good and gracious reign over all things has begun in the life, death, and resurrection of Jesus, but is not yet completed.

Laudato Si': Pope Francis (1936–) and St. Francis of Assisi (1181/2–1226)

In March 2013, the College of Cardinals of the Catholic Church elected then Archbishop of Buenos Aires, Argentinian Jorge Mario Bergoglio, Supreme Pontiff, or Pope. Bergoglio chose Francis for his name as pope, after the thirteenth-century founder of the Franciscan order, St. Francis of Assisi. St. Francis has served as a model for the current pope, as he has served, in numerous ways, for many Christians in the nine hundred years following his life.

As a young man of twelfth- and thirteenth-century Assisi, Italy, Francis was not particularly religious. Yet while he was praying one day in a secluded old chapel, he heard God say to him, "Go, Francis, and repair my house which is falling into ruin." Francis was certain that God was speaking to him, although he was not sure what God was saying. He came to understand God's call to him as a call to embrace God's project of shalom and to assist the church to own God's project as the church's primary project as well.

Born into a wealthy Italian family, by some accounts Francis responded to God's call rather dramatically, abandoning his family's status and prosperity and his lavish and carefree youth. In its place, he embraced a life of poverty in order to identify with Jesus and to minister to the poor and the sick. In its place, he came to regard all of God's creation as his family. As Pope Benedict XVI, the immediate predecessor of Pope Francis, put it, the house Jesus told Francis to rebuild "was first of all his own life, which needed repair through authentic conversion; it was the Church, not the one made of stones but living persons, always needing purification; it was all of humanity, in whom God loves to dwell."[11] So Francis went to work, repairing his own life with his commitment to share the riches of the gospel, to build a community of the poor in spirit to minister to others, near and far, and to live in peace not only with his fellow friars but with all of creation.

Pope Francis, it seems, has heard his own call to rebuild the house, and much like St. Francis he has enthusiastically undertaken that work. "My people are poor and I am one of them," he is frequently quoted as saying, and in his first week as pope he proclaimed, "How I wish for a Church that is poor and for the poor."[12] Like his namesake, Pope Francis has opted for a simplicity of life unusual for one of his high office,

---

11. Pope Benedict XVI, "Angelus," Saint Peter's Square, Sunday, October 22, 2006.
12. Pentin, "Pope," para. 5.

living in an apartment rather than in the papal palace, cooking his own meals, traveling around Rome in his old car and on public transport, and walking about in old shoes as he greets and blesses the poor and the sick as well as the rich and powerful. Only very small and insignificant things, the humble pontiff would no doubt profess.

Jorge Mario Bergoglio was born into a middle-class family, and as a young man he trained to be a chemical technician. After working in a lab for only a short while, at the age of twenty-one Jorge Mario left for seminary; three years later he entered the Society of Jesus, the order of the Jesuits, a religious order known for its educational efforts and dedicated to the care of the whole person, seeking "to nurture men and women for others." Jorge Mario was ordained a priest in 1969. He served briefly as a college professor before he was appointed in 1973 a Provincial, an administrator for Jesuit activities in Argentina. After six years, he returned to university life and served as a parish priest. In May 1992, Pope John Paul II named him a bishop. In 1998, he was named the archbishop of Buenos Aires, and in 2001 he was created a cardinal, roles he held until his election as pope.

Pope Francis has not been the bureaucrat that some may have expected given his earlier experience. He has puzzled many, especially those not of the Christian faith, as he has held fast to traditional church doctrine and practice and yet with openness and humility has regarded those who have failed to live as the church teaches. His warmth and his care for others are apparent in his proclamation of December 2015–November 2016 an Extraordinary Jubilee Year of Mercy, as the pope hoped for the year to be for all Christians "a true moment of encounter with the mercy of God . . . A living experience of the closeness of the Father, whose tenderness is almost tangible, so that the faith of every believer may be strengthened and thus testimony to [the mercy of God] be ever more effective."[13] Pope Francis continues, "The forgiveness of God cannot be denied to one who has repented, especially when that person approaches the Sacrament of Confession with a sincere heart in order to obtain reconciliation with the Father." God's love extends to all.

In his first encyclical of which he is the sole author (much of Pope Francis's first encyclical, *Lumen Fidei*, was written by Pope Benedict and revised and reworked before it was released by Pope Francis), Pope Francis returned to another theme of his namesake, God's care for his creation and the harmony and unity of persons and the created world

---

13. Francis, "Letter of His Holiness."

that God desires.[14] *The Little Flowers of St. Francis*, a fourteenth-century collection of stories about St. Francis, tells numerous stories of Francis's friendship with God's creation—of Francis preaching to the birds, for example, and of his conversion of the wolf of Gubbio that had been terrorizing the people of that town. St. Francis's love for God's creation is sung most clearly in his "Canticle of Brother Sun," included in *The Little Flowers* and paraphrased in the early twentieth century by the English vicar William Henry Draper as "All Creatures of our God and King":

> All creatures of our God and King,
> lift up your voice and with us sing:
> alleluia, alleluia!
>
> O burning sun with golden beam,
> and shining moon with silver gleam,
> O praise him, O praise him,
> alleluia, alleluia, alleluia!
>
> O rushing wind so wild and strong,
> white clouds that sail in heaven along,
> alleluia, alleluia!
>
> New rising dawn in praise rejoice;
> you lights of evening find a voice:
> O praise him, O praise him,
> alleluia, alleluia, alleluia!
>
> Cool flowing water, pure and clear,
> make music for your Lord to hear:
> alleluia, alleluia!
>
> Fierce fire, so masterful and bright,
> providing us with warmth and light.
> O praise him, O praise him,
> alleluia, alleluia, alleluia!
>
> Earth ever fertile, day by day
> bring forth your blessings on our way;
> alleluia, alleluia!
>
> All flowers and fruits that in you grow,
> let them his glory also show;
> O praise him, O praise him,
> alleluia, alleluia, alleluia!

14. A papal encyclical is a document written by a pope addressing some major issue of the church and intended to educate primarily, but not only, church leaders. *Laudato Si'*, addressing global climate change and its harms, is written to a broader audience.

All you who are of tender heart,
forgiving others, take your part;
alleluia, alleluia!

All you who pain and sorrow bear,
praise God and on him cast your care;
O praise him, O praise him,
alleluia, alleluia, alleluia!

Let all things their Creator bless,
and worship him in humbleness,
alleluia, alleluia!

Praise, praise the Father, praise the Son,
and praise the Spirit, Three in One:
O praise him, O praise him,
alleluia, alleluia, alleluia!

Laudato Si' (*On Care for our Common Home*) was released by the Vatican in May 2015. It is striking in its sense of urgency and conviction that global climate change threatens our world and especially the poor of our world. Francis is not reluctant to identify human sin as the root of all our environmental problems, and that sin manifests itself not only in our slavery to consumption but also in our "technocratic" mindset. Our "Sister, Mother Earth," as St. Francis called her, "now cries out to us because of the harm we have inflicted on her by our irresponsible use and abuse of the goods with which God has endowed her. We have come to see ourselves as her lords and masters, entitled to plunder her at will. The violence present in our hearts, wounded by sin, is also reflected in the symptoms of sickness evident in the soil, in the water, in the air and in all forms of life."[15] Given our sin and the violence in our hearts, we require repentance and an "ecological conversion" so that "the effects of [our] encounter with Jesus Christ become evident in [our] relationship with the world around [us]. Living our vocation to be protectors of God's handiwork is essential to a life of virtue; it is not an optional or a secondary aspect of our Christian experience."[16]

To that end, Pope Francis encourages us to emulate St. Francis, "the example par excellence of care for the vulnerable and of an integral ecology lived out joyfully and authentically." Francis, the pope notes, "was particularly concerned for God's creation and for the poor and outcast. He loved and was deeply loved for his joy, his generous

15. Franics, *Laudato Si'*, #2.
16. Francis, *Laudato Si'*, #217.

self-giving, his openheartedness. He was a mystic and a pilgrim who lived in simplicity and in wonderful harmony with God, with others, with nature and with himself. He shows us just how inseparable the bond is between concern for nature, justice for the poor, commitment to society and interior peace."[17]

We are on a journey, a pilgrimage to God's new Jerusalem, "in which each creature, resplendently transfigured, will take its rightful place and have something to give those poor men and women who will have been liberated once and for all."[18] In closing, Pope Francis encourages us "to sing as we go," never letting our struggles and concerns for our fragile planet destroy the joy of our hope in God.

Put Down the Phone: For Further Thought

1. Identify the traits commonly associated with God, the perfect being. What does it mean for God to be omnipotent, and what are the implications of this for morality and other values and for the kind of world God creates? What are the implications of God's omnipotence for forgiveness?

2. Can you identify any problems with the claim that X (some action) is good or right because/if God wills it? What are these problems?

3. Can you identify any problems with the claim that God wills X (some action) because/if it is good or right? What are these problems?

4. Read the story of Abraham and Isaac in Genesis 22. What kind of God might command someone to sacrifice his son (especially given that this God had promised to bless all nations through this son)? How do you make sense of this?

5. Would you admire Abraham more or would you admire him less if he had stood up to God and said, "No can do! This is my son! Slay me, but I will not slay my son"? Why or why not?

6. Explain how real, and not just imaginary, wrong must take place before forgiveness is possible on the account given here. Can you think of any problems with this account?

7. Could someone want not to be forgiven? Is it possible to forgive someone who wants not to be forgiven?

17. Francis, *Laudato Si'*, #10.
18. Francis, *Laudato Si'*, #243.

8. Could someone want not to be forgiven by God? Is it possible for God to forgive someone who wants not to be forgiven? What would a loving and holy God do with such a person?

9. The account of forgiveness given here leans hard on the language of wrong being done. What is the difference between *wrong being done* or *being wronged* and *harm being done* or *being harmed*? Do you think it is more helpful to unpack forgiveness in the language of harm or wrong? Can any action be harmful and yet not wrong? Can any action be wrong and yet not harmful?

10. Some thinkers believe that one can be wronged only if one has a moral right not to have the wrongful action done to one. What do you think a moral right is, if there is such a thing? Do you think actions are morally wrong because they violate a moral right an individual possesses? Or could one wrong another despite that person lacking any relevant moral right?

11. How do you think the belief that God is a Redeemer who aims at shalom in God's creative, redemptive, sustaining, restoring, and re-creating activities might make a difference for how we understand living well? How could that tell us anything about what we are to be or do?

12. Do you think Pope Francis is right that "the vocation to be protectors" of God's creation is "essential to a life of virtue"? What else do you think is essential to a life of virtue?

13. Pope Francis claims that there is an "inseparable . . . bond between concern for nature, justice for the poor, commitment to society and interior peace." What do you think he is thinking in claiming this?

7

FROM CHRIST TO THE WORLD

God's Project, Our Nature, and Our Cares

In chapter 5, we discussed the Christian confession that God is the Creator of the heavens and earth and found that belief to ground some type of value realism or value objectivism, the view that there are genuine, real values and truths about values to be discovered by persons. Given what Christians believe about God (as well as what many of us believe about the world), what is valuable and what is worthy is not simply a matter of what you and I feel is valuable. To live well, we should attempt to discover, to recognize, what God values and recognizes to be of worth, what is genuinely valuable and worthy. In creating the universe and seeing that the creation is good, God recognizes what is there, present in the world God has created. That goodness of creation, that shalom, includes what we speak of as moral goodness, as what is fitting and appropriate for human beings, and it includes much more than just moral goodness. The goodness of creation includes truth and beauty and human flourishing and a harmony of all things with one another. That goodness of the creation does not depend upon your or my invention. You and I are creators neither of truth, nor beauty, nor moral goodness. Obedience to God was morally required of Adam and Eve because, given their natures and given God's nature, God was worthy of their love and faithful response; obedience to a perfectly good and loving being is a fitting response to God. And the same is true for us, the children of Adam and Eve, and our love and faithful responses.

In chapter 6, we looked at some moral implications of the Christian confession that God is *for* us, that God is Creator and Redeemer, and we discussed some of God's redemptive activity. God is *for* us and *for* creation and because of this God is active in healing, forgiving, restoring, and re-creating the universe so that we and all of God's creation may live in fellowship with God and with one another. God's ground project in loving, sustaining, and redeeming the world should inform our ground projects.

In this chapter we turn to God's activity in our lives, to God's work of sanctification, to God's remaking us into what God originally intended us to be, God's work of making us into new creations as part of God's project of creating a new heaven and a new earth. We reflect upon our human condition and our dependence upon God to enable and equip us to live in right relationship with God and all that God has created. We consider God's working in us so that we might love, will, and do in a fitting response to God's activity and projects in the world.

7.1 CHRISTIANITY AND HUMAN NATURE

Earlier, we discussed the Christian belief that things in our world are not the way they are supposed to be. We humans are not the way we are supposed to be. We fail to love persons and things fittingly; as Augustine argued, we are inclined to use God and to use other persons—our friends, our spouses, as well as our enemies—rather than to love them as they are worthy of being loved. And we are inclined to love things created by God with a kind of love that is most appropriately directed to persons or to God. Our misdirected loves color and shape all that we want and all that we do, including our quest to know and to value and to feel and do what we should. We need a shot of redemption, and much more than a shot of redemption. We need healing. We need restoration. We need re-creation in order for us to love well, to will and to do as we should. Our third thesis about God and values addresses the work God does in us in order for us to be the sorts of persons God wants us to be, the sorts of persons we ought to be, given our natures and given God's grand ground project.

> Thesis 3: Only when our minds and hearts are functioning properly can we know and love and live in a manner fully appropriate to our natures; only with the assistance of God, with God directing and correcting us, do our minds and hearts function properly.

Christians encounter a God who is perfect and who is thus worthy of our love, a God who is good and who has created a good universe, one who has created an order that bends toward justice and shalom. The Christian encounter with the gracious and loving God originates in the (at least somewhat) accurate perception of one's own moral condition, in our realization that things are not the way they are supposed to be, and that includes us. We do not love God and all that God has created as we should, and the good that, at our best, we would like to do we do not do (see Rom 7:14–25). Not only do we fail to perceive the deep goodness of God's creation, we perceive neither the enormity nor the real nature of evil and wickedness in the world. But we do perceive enough of the goodness of God and God's creation and enough evil to drive us to the loving arms of God. Having received God's grace and God's forgiveness and having embraced God's project of shalom as our own, our minds are illuminated and our hearts softened. Christians begin to see persons and the world with a newfound clarity. We are being transformed, and so we begin to feel with a sympathy not previously available to us.[1] Our hearts and minds, through the healing power of love and forgiveness, begin to function more properly, more as God originally created them to function, thus placing us more in touch with God, and more in touch with ourselves and others and the world in which we live.

What we see when we clearly and accurately see our own character and nature may be painful and shameful to us, but this painful recognition may contribute to both religious awareness and moral growth. Failure to recognize our own sin and our guilt before God prevents us from seeing well and responding appropriately to our world. In G. K. Chesterton's detective story "The Secret of Father Brown," an American visitor presses Father

---

1. At this point (indeed, at almost every point in this chapter) we do well to remember C. S. Lewis's *Mere Christianity*, and especially his discussion, "Nice People or New Men" in the final section of that book. Lewis reminds us that the sight and the sympathy God makes available to those in whom God is working does not obliterate, but respects, our natural character and sensibilities. We are not identical to one another in sight and sympathy prior to our experience with God, nor is that experience of God a great leveler, leaving us all looking and feeling from the exact same place on the platform. Rather, those who are sour and churlish before they encounter God will improve, but they will not suddenly stand alongside those who are further along the way of kindness. Some, graced by God with a natural kindness and charity, although they may not sing the God met in Christ, nevertheless stand closer to Christ-like charity than do some of Christian faith and confession. But, as Lewis suggests in *The Four Loves*, we should distinguish between *nearness to God as likeness to God* and *nearness as approach to God*. It may well be that some who do not confess Christ are closer to God, more like God in terms of their virtues or traits of character. Paradoxically, in terms of their pilgrimage to God, in terms of approach to God, they may stand further from God than some sour and churlish Christian folk.

Brown, a Catholic priest, to disclose the secret of how he solves all the puzzling and mysterious crimes he investigates. The American wants to know
the scientific method Father Brown uses. Father Brown, however, denies
that he has a scientific method, for science is a matter of standing outside
and looking clearly and objectively at things. Brown's method, by contrast, is
a matter of getting inside the criminal, of "thinking his thoughts, wrestling
with his passions; till I have bent myself into the posture of his hunched and
peering hatred; till I see the world with his bloodshot and squinting eyes . . .
Till I am really a murderer."[2] This he describes as a religious exercise, not a
scientific method. The priest continues,

> No man's really any good till he knows how bad he is, or might
> be; till he's realized exactly how much right he has to all this
> snobbery, and sneering, and talking about "criminals," as if they
> were apes in a forest ten thousand miles away; till he's got rid of
> all the dirty self-deception of talking about low types and defi-
> cient skulls; till he's squeezed out of his soul the last drop of the
> oil of the Pharisees; till his only hope is somehow or other to
> have captured one criminal, and kept him safe and sane under
> his own hat.[3]

The painful recognition, Father Brown claims, is the recognition that we are
equals to the criminals we detest and feel superior to. Father Brown suggests
that Christians, when they see and feel rightly, will recognize themselves
as "criminals" much like any other criminals. With the grace of God, we
may capture that criminal that *is* us, that part of us that turns us away from
God and our neighbors, and we may keep that criminal in chains. Nevertheless, a criminal lies within each of us, a part of us that needs capturing
and constraining. What the Christian sees and feels when seeing and feeling
properly is that before God we are all, ever and always, sinners, ever and
always incapable of seeing and loving and doing all the good that God so
much desires and that we and the world need.

7.2 A FIRST MISTAKEN INFERENCE FROM THE VIRTUE OF HUMILITY

Christians think humility, a humility based upon our recognition of our
true characters, a foundational virtue. Virtues are human excellences, traits
that make us better at living the way we should, qualities possessed by and

---

2. Chesterton, "Secret of Father Brown," in *Father Brown Omnibus*, 639.
3. Chesterton, "Secret of Father Brown," in *Father Brown Omnibus*, 640.

operative in humans who feel and love and act in ways fitting our real nature and the situation in which we find ourselves. Virtues are excellences of character, habits, persistent or fixed traits that dispose us to feel and act *for the good*.[4] The possession of virtues equips and enables us to feel and act fittingly, to live the way we should, given the conditions in which we find ourselves. The virtues are not merely the means toward the end of excellent living, not merely valuable as instruments to a goal external to the virtues. To a significant extent, possession of the virtues *constitutes* human well-being. A virtuous person is someone whose character is not wishy-washy and ever-changing but set, and whose character and identity are shaped by her virtues. This is to say, the virtues help us to do what we ought to do, to feel what we ought to feel, and to see things in the world as we ought to see them, given the sorts of beings we are and given the world we perceive. Much of what it means to be an excellent person is to be one who is characterized by virtues.

For example, a person with the virtue of *courage* has become the sort of person who appreciates and values brave actions and courageous feelings and who is inclined to act bravely, even at a significant cost to herself. She doesn't act or feel courageously only occasionally. Rather, you can bet on her acting courageously and taking pleasure in courageous acting. So it is with other virtues such as compassion, self-control, fairness, kindness, and generosity. To have these virtues is to have stable and lasting dispositions to feel and act in ways that express virtues and that comport well with the various fields of the virtues, the areas of action and feeling in which a particular virtue (or several virtues) is relevant. We can acquire and develop these virtuous traits. They can, with much work, come to characterize our feelings and our actions. And having developed these traits, they help us to be persons who will and do what we ought to. They make us better at being what God means us to be.

It is easier to see how courage, compassion, self-control, fairness, and kindness—and perhaps even generosity—are beneficial traits of character, are virtues, than to understand how the same can be said of humility. This was certainly Aristotle's view.[5] Aristotle's model of moral virtuosity is the magnanimous person, the person with "greatness of soul." The "great-souled person" aims to do noble and great deeds, and she accomplishes these worthy deeds with greatness and nobility. Because of her great ambitions and achievements, she is worthy of great respect and honors, the respect

4. Much of the language here is borrowed from Adams, *Theory of Virtue*, 14.

5. Aristotle's views on magnanimity and humility are insightfully discussed in Rebecca Konyndyk DeYoung's *Vainglory*, 75–85.

of others as well as her own respect for herself. By contrast, "Someone who thinks he is worthy of less than he is worthy of is pusillanimous . . . The pusillanimous person is deficient both in relation to himself [i.e., his worth] and in relation to the magnanimous person's estimate of his own worth. The vain person makes claims that are excessive for himself, [but these same claims would not be excessive for the magnanimous person]."[6]

Humility, as Aristotle sees it, is a cowardliness of character, a refusal to recognize one's true dignity and worth and to strive to achieve great things in light of one's greatness. Those who are characterized by humility always settle for less. Because they settle, not only do they achieve far less than the greatness of the great-souled person, but they fail to recognize their own moral worth. Aristotle is thinking here of people who do not strive to be all they might be, all they are capable of being, and not the servile person, one who fails to understand and acknowledge his own moral rights, letting people trample over him.[7] Still, our common, ordinary view of humility places it very close indeed to servility, perhaps only one step removed from it. We tend to associate humility with self-abasement, with a lack of a sufficiently positive attitude about oneself, and with a reluctance or an inability to recognize what one might achieve if one really tried.

But that is not how Christians historically have understood humility. Instead, Christian thought has started with reflection upon Jesus Christ, true God and true human, and his humility. "Though he was in the form of God, he did not regard equality with God as something to be exploited, but emptied himself, taking the form of a slave, being born in human likeness. And being found in human form, he humbled himself and became obedient to the point of death—even death on a cross" (Phil 2:6–8). Humility expresses our awareness of our comparative need or dependence upon another. Humility is a disposition to defer to one whom we recognize as equal to us or greater than we are in some relevant respect. As St. Benedict suggested in his "rule" that has guided and inspired Christian monasticism since the fifth century, we must travel through humility—the disposition to recognize who we truly are before God our Creator, Redeemer, and Sustainer—on our way to true greatness of spirit and love of God. We must recognize ourselves, St. Benedict argued, as finite and fallible, always as sinners (although not always sinning), being transformed and remade in Christ's image. We are always in need of healing, always in need of God's precious grace, forgiveness, and sustaining love. This acknowledgment of our dependence upon God is the starting point for obedience to God and

6. Aristotle, *Nicomachean Ethics*, 1123b.

7. See Hill, "Servility and Self-Respect."

for loving God rightly. We climb the ladder of humility to true friendship and love of God, St. Benedict maintained.

Nevertheless, there are two wrong inferences we might make from the powerful affirmation of humility as a virtue, two especially debilitating mistakes we might make if we are not seeing clearly and accurately *the equality of sin* and the corresponding *equality of need for grace* to which humility disposes us. These mistakes undercut moral seriousness and undermine our trying to think carefully about doing and feeling what we should and our trying to live well in light of our reflections about what we should do and who we should try to be.

The first mistaken inference has to do with the making of moral judgments in light of humility's recognition of the equality of sin, that is, that in some respect my sin is as great as the sin of any other person; all of us depend upon God, all of us need the healing and help of God. If we are all equal in sin, then no one is in a position to make moral judgments, or so some people argue.

Recall Father Brown's suggestion that we are equals in sin in that we all have a criminal within us. Having observed the criminal within themselves, some Christians conclude that the whole task of reflection upon values and who and what we should try to be, and the exploration of the pursuit of goodness and living well, is mistaken. Given our condition, they maintain, our hope must be in God alone, for our efforts to capture and constrain our sin will always fall short. We would do better just to skip the attention to how we live and, instead, to focus all our efforts on understanding and loving God, who brings healing to us. We would more wisely come to God only confessing the criminals we know ourselves to be. That, they claim, is the path of humility.

By contrast, they suggest that the path of moral reflection and moral seriousness and the pursuit of a good life leads inevitably to the arrogance and pride that Aristotle appeared to champion. Didn't Jesus discourage that route? Didn't Jesus condemn the moral comparison of oneself and others in which we find the others morally lacking? Jesus taught, "Do not judge, so that you may not be judged" (Matt 7:1–5; Luke 6:37–38). If humility disposes us to see ourselves as we truly are, to see that our sin is equal to that of others, if we are all sinners, then in what position are we to judge whether someone else's lying or cheating is wrong? Given that we are not morally perfect ourselves, from what vantage point do we dare judge the actions of others, as though we are their moral superiors? But isn't that what moral reflection, what moral seriousness encourages? Isn't it far better to follow Jesus' teaching and to refrain from judging the actions and characters of others as right or wrong, good or bad? Better not to judge others at all, they claim.

You and I should, by all means, take seriously the teaching of Jesus, but that requires us, first of all, to be sure that we understand his teaching. Two considerations are especially relevant as we try to make sense of this difficult teaching, "Do not judge . . ." The first is that in his teaching Jesus typically made use of hyperbole and exaggeration in making his points, and the context of the "Do not judge . . ." passage in Matthew's gospel illustrates this well. Notwithstanding *The Guinness Book of Records* or *Ripley's Believe It or Not*, no one can live with a log in her eye—a log won't really fit in your eye (Matt 7:3; Luke 6:42). But the contrasting images of an eye with a tiny speck of dust in it and an eye with a log in it make clear that it won't do to treat equals differently, to apply different standards to others than to oneself. Jesus' message, when we read the "Do not judge . . ." verse in context (whether in Matthew or in Luke), powerfully says that there is a spiritual and moral danger attached to exempting oneself from the moral standards to which one holds others, in thinking oneself superior to others. Each of us desperately needs God's grace and forgiveness. When it comes to loving God and loving our neighbors as we should, the safe bet is that you and I need God's forgiveness every bit as much as any of our neighbors. The problem is with having different standards for oneself and others, not with judging, not with moral reflection and moral seriousness.

A second consideration in interpreting Jesus' "Do not judge . . ." is to note Jesus' own actions with respect to the teaching in question. Jesus himself was a sensitive and perceptive judge of the sins of others. Matthew's gospel includes not only Jesus' judgment upon those who were abusing the temple but numerous instances of "Woe to you because you are doing evil things" as well. And he counseled his disciples and followers to discern, discriminate, and judge. "If another member of the church sins against you, go and point out the fault when the two of you are alone" (Matt 18:15). Recognizing that another has sinned against you is an act of judging, of moral evaluation. Indeed, as Jesus implies, forgiveness will be able to get off the ground only if you and the person who seeks forgiveness from you agree, more or less, in judging some word or action or disposition or feeling as wrong and agree in your similar evaluations of the gravity of the wrong done or the tendency to feel and act wrongly.

Although we ought to be attentive lest we find ourselves confident that we can earn our salvation on the basis of our good works, and although we ought to be on guard lest our moral reflection and concern lead us from an appropriate humility, this does not rule out taking morality and other values seriously. The equality of sin does not preclude our appropriately attending to the moral character of actions and assessing them for their rightness or wrongness, their goodness or evil. We ought not to apply a different set of standards to others than that which we apply to ourselves; we ought not to judge others more harshly than we judge ourselves. Nor should our judgments ever declare individuals beyond the pale of God's reach. That would be presumption indeed! Rather, as we attempt to think and live faithfully in response to God's action in the world we should attempt to discern in our own actions, emotions, and dispositions—and in the actions, emotions, and dispositions of others—that which is good, and right, and pure, and holy, and just. "Finally, beloved, whatever is true, whatever is honorable, whatever is just, whatever is pure, whatever is pleasing, whatever is commendable, if there is any excellence and if there is anything worthy of praise, think about these things" (Phil 4:8).

7.3 A SECOND MISTAKEN INFERENCE FROM THE VIRTUE OF HUMILITY

The first mistaken inference from the recognition that humility is a virtue for Christians is that if we are humble, we will recognize the equality of sin, that we are never in a position to judge others, for there will always be a log in our eye. Therefore, for the sake of morality, for the sake of humility, we ought not to judge others, we ought not to take the moral life and living well seriously. To engage in reflection upon morality and other values, to identify what actions are right or wrong, good or bad, is the way of pride and arrogance, that is, the way of moral vices, this mistaken argument concludes.

A second wrong inference from the recognition that humility is a virtue also leads to a refusal to attend seriously to values and to moral issues and to care about one's moral character and actions. It arrives at this conclusion in one of two ways: either by *resignation to sin* or by *libertinism*, to use language that is probably not a part of your everyday vocabulary. These are importantly different from our first mistake, which encouraged us to abandon moral reflection in order to be more moral, in order to be genuinely humble.

First, let's think about *resignation to sin*. Some Christians minimize the importance of taking the moral life seriously because, they claim, it will do us little good. It is not time well spent, for we just can't accomplish very much morally. We humans are equals in sin, and the sin of each of us is so great that our progress as pilgrims will be only infinitesimal. Better just to preach Christ and Christ crucified for our sins. Others argue that taking morality seriously, the very attempt to accomplish anything morally, is hubris, a failure to be humble and to recognize that all good comes from God. To take morality seriously, they argue, is to begin to trust in one's own abilities rather than to rely upon the merciful guidance of God. Thus, even to attempt to accomplish something morally is *not* to accomplish much morally because the very attempt is inevitably tainted. Better to live ever mindful of our dependence upon God, attempting little, accomplishing little, and resigned to our nature as sinners until we are made perfect by God. Better to live prayerfully, ever mindful that it is not our own work but God's work in us to accomplish God's aims, for we sinful humans are likely just to make a bigger mess of things.

Some other Christians (especially Lutheran Christians, in my experience) argue that what the risen Christ gives to us is permission, is freedom to live fully in the confidence that God has forgiven us, and that the God *for* us will never turn against us. To grasp that we are equals in our sin before God, that we all harbor a criminal within, is, they argue, to be empowered to act boldly, knowing that God is merciful and will forgive anything and everything that needs forgiving. We are set free by Christ, now at liberty to live with courage, confidence, and zeal. To think carefully about the moral life and living well is to live timidly, is to fail to live as people who have been set free by Christ, to live as those who dare, because of Christ, to sin boldly.

Of course, neither *resignation to sin* nor *libertinism* follows from humility and our clear sight about the equality of our sinful characters. As Father Brown suggests, *contra libertinism*, the criminal within each of us must be captured, and part of the work of moral reflection is to help us capture and "keep safe and sane" the criminal within us. Furthermore, as Father Brown suggests, *contra resignation*, the criminal within us *can* be captured, more or less. Both *resignation* and *libertinism* permit the criminal within us to roam too freely, either because we cannot fully contain him or because "Christ sets the prisoners free." Both ignore the harm that the unconstrained criminal within us may do to others or to ourselves.[8]

7.4 GOD'S GRACE AND PROPER FUNCTIONING

A critical insight gained from our encounter with God is the great wideness of God's mercy, the extensiveness and the steadfastness of God's goodness and grace toward us and the breadth and depth of our own poor health, our

---

8. And both encourage us, suggests Eucharistic Prayer C of Rite 2 of the Episcopal Church USA, to approach the Eucharist, or Holy Communion, wrongly. We pray, "Deliver us from the presumption of coming to this Table for solace only, and not for strength; for pardon only, and not for renewal."

feeling and doing wrong and our tendency to feel and do less than what is good for us, for others, and for God's creation. We depend upon God for life and for our healing. In our experience of God, we gain a vision of a God who loves and travels to meet *every* sinner. It isn't helpful to level all sin or sinners beyond this point. The equality of sinners—that all of us stand alienated from God and in need of God's forgiving grace—does not entail the equality of the sins we commit. Some of us sin more than others, and frankly, some of our sins are more harmful and damaging to others and to God's creation than other sins. If the good life is concerned with our living well with one another, and living well as the sorts of creatures we are, then even though all of us fall short of living as we should, some of the actions of some of us at least some of the time are far more detrimental to our lives together than other actions.[9] At the level of my need for God's forgiveness for my sins of not loving God as I should, I may be equal to a murderer; I am no less in need of forgiveness and help than he or she. But at the moral level of the impact of my acts upon others or upon God's creation, I am not equal to the murderer, for I've not murdered anyone.[10] It is better for the world that I not be a murderer, better for the world that you not be a murderer, better that we all recognize that no matter how much we stand in the need of God, some of us have acted in ways more harmful to others than others of us have, and that some of us are more guilty than others of lives and actions destructive of the shalom of God's project.

How do we reconcile our common, everyday sense that some actions really are worse than others with our Christian conviction that we are all guilty and in need of God's grace? As God works in our lives, the clear sight and proper feeling God gives to us enables us to see the need of all for reconciliation and transformation. We recognize that we, like others, constantly fail to love God, each other, and God's creation as we should. With God's aid, we remember that God is always for us. We needn't believe that we are all equally sinful, though we are all equals in that we are sinners. It needn't matter much to us who are the greater and lesser sinners. Not loving God well and not loving others and God's creation as we should characterizes each of us, however "great" or however "small" our sins may be. Beyond

9. Reinhold Niebuhr's way of putting this point is that there is an "equality of sin" and an "inequality of guilt." Guilt, as Niebuhr construes it, is "the objective consequence of sin." More helpfully, guilt is "the actual corruption of the plan of creation and providence in the historical world." See Niebuhr, *Nature and Destiny of Man*, vol. 1, 219–27.

10. Of course, things are more complicated than this. Perhaps the only reason I've not murdered anyone is that I've had the good luck not to be in conditions in which I might have the wherewithal and the temptation to murder. On moral luck, see Nagel, "Moral Luck." For a much different perspective, see Zagzebski, "Religious Luck."

this, some people outdo you and me in doing good, while others outdo us in doing evil. This recognition is crucial, for, as Reinhold Niebuhr puts it, "the difference between a little more and a little less justice in a social system and between a little more and a little less selfishness in the individual may represent differences between sickness and health, between misery and happiness in particular situations."[11] In other words, although each of us needs dance lessons—for none of us is the dance partner God deserves—it doesn't follow from this that no one dances any better than anyone else. Nor does it follow that we needn't try to dance just because we won't be good partners or that we need not practice dancing just because we won't ever get it perfectly right. Nor should it matter who the best dancer is and who is the worst. Each of us is called to dance well with God and with other persons and with all of God's creation. Each of us needs healing in order to dance well. God is for us; the healing has begun. Let's dance.

Is the attempt to take values and morality seriously sometimes a sinful thing? No doubt about it. The temptation to think better of ourselves than we think of others and better than we deserve to think of ourselves is always with us, and taking values and the moral life seriously surely presents us with numerous temptations to think better of ourselves than of others and to think better of ourselves than is fitting and appropriate. Hypocrisy is a vice, and we, almost all of us, are hypocrites. (And people, for whatever reason, tend to find the hypocrisy of religious believers especially offensive.)

The alternative of not taking our moral characters seriously is hardly preferable. To have encountered God, to be aware of God's abundant goodness to us, and to have our hearts moved to love God is to want to respond in the appropriate and fitting way to God's great mercy and the value of our lives and the world God has created. To love God is to want to learn to love what God loves, is to want to see the world as God sees it, is to want to live, here and now, as the sort of creature God wants one to be. To love God is, in short, to care about how one lives, is to care about God's projects, and to want our own projects to share in God's projects. To love God is to care about living a good life, for, as Irenaeus suggested, the glory of God is humans living fully as the persons God created us to be.

And to love God is to recognize that God is working in our lives, making us to be new creations so that we can love and live as God wants us to do. God begins the work of sanctification within us, Christians believe. Having forgiven us, having restored us to a right relationship, God comes to us in the Holy Spirit to sustain the good work of God within us, and to heal and to guide us in the ways of God. "Do not be conformed to the world, but be

11. Niebuhr, *Nature and Destiny of Man*, vol. 1, 220.

transformed by the renewing of your minds, so that you may discern what is the will of God—what is good and acceptable and perfect," Paul writes to the church in Rome (Rom 12:2). And he has "not ceased praying for you," he assures the Christians in Colossae, "that you may be filled with the knowledge of God's will in all spiritual wisdom and understanding, so that you may lead lives worthy of the Lord, fully pleasing to him, as you bear fruit in every good work and as you grow in the knowledge of God" (Col 1:9–10). The hope, the confident expectation of Christians is that our healing has begun and that with that our hearts and minds are being corrected, restored to more proper functioning so that, despite our natures, we can see more clearly what God is calling us to do, and we can follow God more nearly and love God more dearly. This is the work that God has begun and continues as we walk in faith with God.

Christians are those who recognize that they have been created by God to be partners in a dance, who have been invited and equipped so to dance, and who have thus joined God's dance. They have recognized the goodness and beauty of God's creation and have recognized a goodness in God and creation which they have not loved fittingly and well. Christians are those who, having encountered God, have begun to see the truth about the way the world is supposed to be and the way the world currently is. Having encountered a gracious God, Christians turn away from the world's sin and evil, turn away from their rebellion against God, and turn to Christ. Because the creation, although fallen and distorted, is nevertheless in some sense good and created by God for the purpose of shalom—because God in Christ is at work restoring and re-creating the world for the promised shalom—the Christian makes not only the first movement of repentance and renunciation away from the world and toward God, but a second movement as well, a God-directed movement from Christ (back) to the world.

That God's creation is good, that creatures created in the image of God are worthy of respect and honor because of their nature and God's intentions for the world and not just because *we* happen to believe them worthy of respect and honor, are essential components in a proper Christian understanding and love of the world. Christians do flee from a sinful world into the arms of God. But this God in whose arms we find ourselves sends us back to a world created good, a world that God has not abandoned and has promised never to abandon. God believes that the created order is worthy of ongoing love and care. God calls us to God's grand ground project of shalom, an end made possible by the death and resurrection of Jesus the Christ. God, in the Holy Spirit, directs our loving and willing and acting in concert with God's loving, willing, and acting. The Holy Spirit guides us in the dance as we follow the lead of God the Creator and Redeemer of all.

This is what the Christian begins to see rightly and well, what the lost Christian begins to see as she starts to find her way. This is what she begins to learn to love as her own goal and as her own good, in receiving the healing love of God. The Christian life is a dance in which we seek to follow the lead of a gracious and forgiving God, a God who accomplishes God's project and purposes in creation with us, despite our wandering and weak steps.

Jonathan Edwards (1703–58)

America's greatest "homegrown" philosopher and theologian is known to most Americans (if he is known at all) as the Puritan preacher of "Sinners in the Hands of an Angry God"—not the type of sermon that immediately comes to mind when one thinks about someone aptly described as a theologian of beauty. This sermon that Edwards wrote and preached vividly depicts the sinner dangling over the fires of hell, much as a spider might be dangled over a campfire by a child. Will the spider fall into the fiery flames? Will the sinner repent, or will he fall into the fires of hell?

Jonathan Edwards, in fact, was probably as fascinated with the dangling of spiders from their webs as he was fearful for the fate of unrepentant sinners. Born in Connecticut in 1703, the son of a minister, Edwards grew up intimately aware of, fascinated by, and in love with the natural world. As a twenty-year-old he penned a letter, complete with illustrations, intricately describing the swinging movement of the spider in spinning its web. He concluded from his observations, "Hence the exuberant goodness of the Creator, who hath not only provided for all the necessities, but also for the pleasure and recreation of all sorts of creatures, even the insects."[12] God's care for the world and the beauty of God's creation is present in even the smallest details of the universe.

In his "Personal Narrative," Edwards tells of the gradual development in his consciousness of an "inward, sweet delight in God and divine things."[13] On one memorable occasion, as he walked alone in his father's pasture,

> The appearance of everything was altered; there seemed to
> be, as it were, a calm, sweet cast, or appearance of divine glory,
> in almost everything. God's excellency, his wisdom, his purity
> and love, seemed to appear in everything; in the sun, moon, and

---

12. Edwards, "The 'Spider' Letter," 167.
13. Edwards, "Personal Narrative," 792.

stars; in the clouds, and blue sky; in the grass, flowers, trees; in the water, and all nature. . . . I often used to sit and view the moon for a long time; and so in the daytime, spent much time in viewing the clouds and sky, to behold the sweet glory of God in these things; in the meantime, singing forth with a low voice my contemplations of the Creator and Redeemer. And scarce anything, among all the works of nature, was so sweet to me as thunder and lightning. . . . I felt God at the first appearance of a thunderstorm. And used to take the opportunity . . . to fix myself in order to view the clouds, and see the lightnings play, and hear the majestic and awful voice of God's thunder . . . leading me to sweet contemplations of my great and glorious God. And while I viewed, used to spend my time, as it always seemed natural to me, to sing, or chant forth my meditations; to speak my thoughts in soliloquies with a singing voice.[14]

The heart moved (to sing) by God's beauty and the beauty of God's creation, the "inward, sweet delight" in beauty and goodness, was central in Edwards's moral theory. Moral goodness, or virtue, in Edwards's terms, "consists in benevolence to Being in general." Edwards continues, "Or perhaps to speak more accurately, it [true virtue] is that consent, propensity and union of heart to Being in general, that is immediately exercised in a general good will."[15]

Here's what I think Edwards meant: When one has an authentic encounter with God and recognizes her own sin before God, not only does God grant forgiveness, in the Holy Spirit God offers us new hearts, new loves, a new inward sense and delight in God and goodness. With this new sense, we can finally begin to see with greater clarity the way things really are. What we see is that God is the best account of everything. What is most real, what is the explanation for everything else that is, is God, or more precisely, the divine activity of the Trinity—Father, Son, and Holy Spirit. Moral excellence, moral virtue, thus consists of seeing things the way they really are and valuing what one sees in the way that is appropriate to the genuine worth of things. Morally virtuous persons love God's projects and plans, and thus try to align themselves with those projects and plans because they are God's and, as such, good in themselves, as well as good for oneself and others.

Edwards's moral theory is, of course, much more complex than this, but his emphasis upon a conversion of the heart and God's gift of

14. Edwards, "Personal Narrative," 793–94.
15. Edwards, *Nature of True Virtue*, 540.

a new "inward sense" through which we see and love God's beauty and the beauty of all that is created by God, see and love and sing the goodness and harmony at the heart of all things, is what is most important at this point. God gives us eyes to see what is good and beautiful. God re-creates within us hearts to love God and God's good and beautiful creation. God gives us mouths to sing God's praise and spirits that cannot keep from singing.

Despite his encounters with God, Edwards's life was not without many sorrows. Edwards believed that the church, as the body of Christ, should have as its members only those who could and would publicly testify to an authentic experience of God. Others in his congregation thought the church should welcome anyone who wants to be a member, regardless of their public testimony. The issue divided his church, and after a vote in which his position was defeated by a majority of one vote, Edwards was asked to leave. Sadly, he moved to the Indian mission in Stockbridge, Massachusetts, and there served two smaller congregations and oversaw a school for Mahican Indian boys. There in Stockbridge he also completed his last major intellectual works, one of them his *Nature of True Virtue* where his mature moral theory is displayed. Edwards died on March 22, 1758, less than five weeks after he had been inaugurated as president of what is now Princeton University, his death resulting from complications from a smallpox inoculation.

Put Down the Phone: For Further Thought

1. What do you think are the greatest moral risks/problems in making moral judgments? What troubles you about making moral judgments?

2. What are the moral risks of not making moral judgments? What if you really tried to live judging not, lest you be judged?

3. How would you respond to someone who said to you, "Studying Christian morality is, at best, a waste of time (and is probably sinful). If you love Jesus and you pray, God will show you what to do and what sort of person to be. All you need to do is study God." (Or, alternatively, "You needn't study Christian ethics; all you need is love.")

4. What is hypocrisy? How bad a thing is it to be a hypocrite? Is there any upside to hypocrisy?

5. Do you think humility is a virtue? Could one who is not a Christian also recognize that humility is a virtue? How so?

6. Identify some additional Christian virtues. Is there any sort of priority among the virtues? That is, are there some virtues we should especially aspire to possess? Or, as human excellences, are they all of equal worth and importance?

7. What do you take to be the implications for punishment, for who we should punish and how we should punish them, of the belief in the equality of sinners?

8. Morality is one of the goods we may pursue, but only one of a number of goods we may embrace as projects. What are some other goods? How do we determine which goods we should embrace as projects, and which goods take priority over others as we seek to lead lives faithful to God?

9. How might Jonathan Edwards's account of a new, inward moral sense explain moral disagreements? Are there any problems with using the new moral sense to explain disagreements? How do we explain moral disagreements between Christians given that all Christians will have received a new moral sense?

8

CHRISTIAN VOCATION, GOODS, AND THE GOOD LIFE

Donaldina "Lo Mo" Cameron (1869–1968)[1]

Separated from her by a span of one hundred and fifty years, we may think our lives very different from that of Donaldina "Dolly" Cameron. Still, her discovery of her vocation, her calling, is not unlike that of most of us. God did not call her as God called Abraham and the Old Testament prophets. Instead, Dolly Cameron planned a life as a teacher, but her plans were interrupted. Like most of us, she stumbled into God's will and, so it might appear, only discovered her vocation by accident. Her life went much differently than she had expected as she tried to trust and follow God's will.

Dolly was born in New Zealand in 1869 to Scottish Presbyterian parents who had immigrated from the highlands of Scotland to New Zealand to raise sheep. Within several years of her birth, her parents and five siblings moved again, this time to America, south of San Francisco, hoping for greener pastures and better ranching in the relatively new state of California. With the completion of the transcontinental railroad in 1869, California was open for business.

1. This material is drawn primarily from Mildred Crowl Martin's *Chinatown's Angry Angel* and Kristin and Kathryn Wong, *Fierce Compassion*.

Opportunities seemed to abound in the western state and many people immigrated to California with dreams of a better life, including scores of native Chinese fleeing to America to escape attacks upon their families by criminal gangs in their homeland. Filled with hopes, perhaps of finding gold, and often lured by the false promises of their "handlers," many Chinese men borrowed money to get to America. Once on American soil, their dreams of easy money vanished, while their debts quickly accumulated. With the decline of the gold rush, these poor and vulnerable Chinese ended up doing menial jobs, taking whatever work they could find—including the hard, dangerous work of building the railroads—doing that which American citizens couldn't or wouldn't do, or wouldn't do so cheaply.

With rampant poverty and with a disproportionate number of Chinese men to women—between 1870 and 1890, only a tiny 4 to 6 percent of the Chinese population in America was female—social problems erupted. Chinese gangs bullied and intimidated many of the male immigrants, using drugs and prostitutes to extend their control over immigrants. An extensive underground trade in sex developed, with immigrant Chinese women kidnapped in China, smuggled into America and sold as slaves to American Chinese men, or sold directly into prostitution. This activity further stoked the hostility of the already angry and worried white Americans. Ostracization of the Chinese, outrage, and fear were the primary responses to the large numbers of Chinese immigrants. The Chinese were forced to live in Chinatowns. And with the worry of American citizens that the Chinese were taking American jobs, and fears that the criminal gangs that had terrorized China would expand beyond these Chinatowns and that the poverty, violence, and sex trade would infect other American communities, the Chinese immigrants were watched closely, through suspicious eyes. A refrain that, sadly, echoes to the present day rang through the streets of San Francisco: "These (Chinese) immigrants are stealing our jobs!"

California had enacted numerous laws in the 1860s to address what were already viewed as social problems of immigration, primarily the sex trade, with some of these laws challenged in the state courts. In 1875, the Page Act was passed by the United States Congress, prohibiting "undesirables," that is to say, almost all Chinese women, from entering the United States. In 1882, the Chinese Exclusion Act banned most Chinese men as well, all except merchants and those of elite professions, from entering the United States. Chinese women were in a double bind. They were victims not only of the slave traders but also of unjust US laws that in punishing the slave traders at the same time deprived these women of their fourteenth amendment rights of life, liberty, and property and due process under the law. Only a few white Americans were attentive to their cries. Donaldina Cameron would become one of those few.

The isolated pioneer life of the Cameron family on the California range was hard. Dolly's mother died when Dolly was five, and her older sisters took on the responsibility of raising her while her father and her brother worked the range. Only a short time after her mother's death, her father's sheep herd was decimated by harsh weather. With no herd and little money, the family sought new opportunities closer to San Francisco and moved again. Dolly graduated from high school and began a teacher training course, but soon after she began those studies, her father died and her future, again, appeared uncertain. Later Dolly fell in love. She was briefly engaged, but only briefly, a story whose ending she would never share with others.

Several years passed, times of some uncertainty about what her future might hold. Then, after many afternoons and evenings hearing a family friend speak of courageous Christian service in Chinatown and the work of the Occidental Mission Home for Girls, Dolly was persuaded by the friend to volunteer for a year at the mission. Unsure of what gifts and abilities she had to offer the mission home in Chinatown dedicated to rescuing young Chinese women from the slave trade and prostitution, but certain of the value of that work, Dolly agreed to volunteer and serve for a year. The twenty-five-year-old moved to San Francisco, to 920 Sacramento Street, to aid Miss Margaret Culbertson and the Occidental Mission Home's work of intervening when young Chinese women called, helping them escape, offering them a safe haven, and educating them and preparing them for a life freed from slavery.

What began as a trial year became a life of service, often extremely risky and dangerous service, to others. On the very day of her arrival at 920 Sacramento Street, Miss Culbertson informed Donaldina that enough sticks of dynamite to blow up a city block had been left that morning on the front porch of the home. Within the month, Donaldina had joined Miss Culbertson, a couple of policemen, and a Chinese interpreter as they used sledgehammers to break into a house to rescue a Chinese girl hidden in a room. For Donaldina, the work had begun, with the curses and the threats that followed the rescues, as well as the day-to-day tasks of loving and caring for badly broken Chinese girls and young women.

Nearing the end of her trial year, the Board of the Occidental Mission Home for Girls asked Donaldina to stay on, so valuable was her assistance to the tireless but frail Miss Culbertson. Dolly took a night to think it over and then agreed to continue her work as Miss Culbertson's right hand. Soon after Dolly's second year with the mission had begun, poor health forced Margaret Culbertson to take a sabbatical rest, and Dolly stepped in as superintendent. When Miss Culbertson suddenly died, a new superintendent of the mission was appointed, and Dolly continued her work of loving and teaching the women and girls of the mission and acting in rescues as needed. But distraught at the death of Miss Culbertson and worried about her own future, Dolly became overwhelmed by the work and found herself in a dark and depressing time. Still, she carried on, loving and being loved by her charges, who gave her the Chinese name Lo Mo, or "old mama." In 1900, thirty-one-year-old Dolly Cameron was appointed superintendent of the mission home.

Again, her life spun around and around before slowing down and settling. In the early 1900s, Dolly fell in love with a friend of her siblings, a young man who felt called to be a Presbyterian minister and to head east across the nation to prepare for the ministry at Princeton Theological Seminary in New Jersey. Their romance was carried on long distance, with each of them doing the work they believed God was calling them to do. In 1904, thirty-five-year-old Dolly traveled to the East Coast to discuss with Charles, her love, how they could marry and each continue to obey God's call. They struggled with the question, and finding no good answer, they parted, both of them brokenhearted yet committed to following God's call. Dolly returned to 920 Sacramento Street and her many "children" at the mission.

She and the mission had endured the bubonic plague of 1900 and the quarantine of Chinatown to contain the plague. They survived the 1906 San Francisco earthquake, which brought the complete destruction of the mission home and, in the chaos following the earthquake, burning and looting in Chinatown. She continued the work of the mission in exile. The slave trade did not rest, and neither would she, certainly not as long as her "children" needed her. In 1908 a new building for the mission was completed at 920 Sacramento Street and the mission returned home.

In April 1911, Donaldina Cameron attended what she believed would be her final annual meeting as the superintendent of the Occidental Mission Home. She had served the mission as superintendent for more than a decade. Much had changed during that time, even while the struggles remained the same. Dolly had grown increasingly troubled and more vocal in her criticism of US immigration laws, believing that the laws discouraged family life and that, in fact, they contributed to the slavery of Chinese women. And she had fallen in love again and planned to be married in July of that year. God, she believed, was calling her to some different field. Then, in a flash, again things changed, and her plans and expectations were upended. She received a telegram informing her of the sudden, unexpected death of her fiancé. Dolly took six months' leave from the mission, but then returned to her work, picking up where she had planned to leave off.

So the years passed, with the Occidental Mission always busy, the home always crowded. The United States entered World War I in 1917. The work of Donaldina Cameron and the mission continued. A little more than a decade later Wall Street crashed and the Great Depression began. The mission, always dependent upon the fundraising skills of the superintendent and the charity of others, struggled to stay afloat. War seemed to erupt in Chinatown, with the Chinese gangs fighting each other in the streets and the Chinatown police having sometimes more success, sometimes less, in subduing them. And the gangs fought not only in the streets but also in the courts, hiring lawyers and suing for custody of girls who had escaped from their grip and were living in the mission home. The Occidental Mission fought back and was successful in some, but not all, of these trials. Their losses were heart-wrenching. At last, in the 1930s, with the aid and the encouragement of Donaldina Cameron and some of the women she had rescued, federal authorities brought charges against a wealthy Chinatown hardware merchant suspected of operating one of the largest rings of the Chinese slave trade. The prosecution in "The Broken Blossoms Case" was successful, and the major artery of the Chinese slave trade was severed. The slave trade never returned to its earlier strength.

Dolly Cameron retired, more or less, when she turned sixty-five. The work of the Occidental Mission turned in new directions. Dolly moved out of 920 Sacramento Street and moved in with her older sisters. She continued to pray, to care for "920" and the work of the mission as she could. The American internment of Japanese civilians in the 1940s, some of whom had been her "children" at 920, deeply distressed her. She prayed, and lived quietly, remembered in gratitude by the many whose lives she had touched, remembering with gratitude God's faithfulness to her throughout her years, despite the hardships she faced—a gratitude evident in the words from Habakkuk that had long hung above her door: "Yet I will rejoice."

> Though the fig tree does not blossom,
>   And no fruit is on the vines;
> Though the produce of the olive fails,
>   And the fields yield no food;
> Though the flock is cut off from the fold,
>   And there is no herd in the stalls,
> Yet I will rejoice in the LORD;
>   I will exult in the God of my salvation.
>
> (Hab 3:17–18)

8.1 WHERE WE'VE BEEN

Let's review the ground we've traversed as we near the end of this journey. We began with the discovery, the unfortunate realization, that when it comes to figuring out what we should do with our lives and who we should try to be, we are much less sure of things than it may appear. Most of us find ourselves lost, no matter who we are, in matters of how we should live and what it means to live well, after even a little reflection. We seem to have more options before us than earlier generations, but these add to the confusion. Hence our project in this book: to get our bearings, to make some progress along the path of how Christians (and other interested persons) should understand the good life in light of Christian identity and our understanding of God and God's projects.

We began our journey (in chapter 2) by thinking about not just having a brand but being a person, a self. What does it mean for any person to have an identity, to be somebody, and how is that different from simply having a certain way of presenting yourself to others? You and I have desires, affections, beliefs, cares, and habits, and among those habits are virtues, fixed dispositions to see the world, to feel and act, in certain ways. Although these are parts or aspects of who we are, we are the sole creators of none of these. Our biology is a contributor, but so are the people and the communities with whom we have been in conversation from our earliest days. And so, too, are we ourselves contributors, shaped though we may be by biology and these communities and conversations. These properties or aspects of our identity operate as we engage the world in thought and act, as we intend and perform actions to achieve our goals. We find ourselves with projects, some of them relying upon other projects, and we create new projects for ourselves in conversation with others. Some of our projects, such as running a half-marathon in under two hours, are short-lived and relatively inconsequential. Other projects, together, express what we believe to be important and good. These ground projects, informed by our loves and cares, propel us into our futures and make our life meaningful to us.[2] To have an identity, to be somebody, is to be a unified and integrated character of desires, loves, beliefs, cares, habits, projects, and ground projects. To be a self is to be a performer not of a bunch of independent and largely unconnected actions, but to be a performer of a coherent life, something like a musical piece that can be interpreted. To be somebody is to have a story of oneself, a narrative in which the pieces fit together and make sense.

Being a Christian self, having a Christian identity, we argued in chapter 3, is to understand one's story as part of a bigger story, a story that includes the stories of others as well, God's story. Living Christianly is responding to and answering God, one's neighbors, and God's creation in performing one's life. Having met a generous and gracious God, Christians want to respond to God in what they desire, in what they believe, in what they feel and do, in their deepest cares and concerns, in the nuts and bolts of their living. They want to live the way God wants them to live, to embrace God's project as their own project. Christians discover God's story, the story of God's ground project of creation, fall, re-creation, and completion, and locate their own stories as a part of that grand narrative (chapter 4), embracing God's ground project as their own.

In chapters 5 through 7, having discussed the basics of what it looks like for Christians to turn away from a world that is not the way it is supposed to be and to turn to God, we looked at the second conversion of Christians, a conversion of Christians back to the world in light of their understanding of God and God's creation of all things and God's great ground project of redemption and re-creation. Since God is good and a good creator, Christians believe that there are real goods in the world, independent of your or my desiring or believing these goods to be real. In themselves, they are good; our believing them to be so does not make them so. God is for us, and God knows what is good and desires that we live good lives, enjoying the good creation. Central to our living well is our caring for shalom, for living in harmony and right relationship with God, with other persons, and with all of God's creation, something God has made possible in the incarnation, death, and resurrection of Jesus. In Jesus, God is making all things new, and as God makes us new—and as we live in harmony and fellowship with God—we begin to see and feel and understand God and God's purposes better. The healing of our loves, our cares, and our affections, as well as our believing and understanding faculties, is underway, and we are equipped by God to live more fittingly as the sorts of creatures we are.

2. Bernard Williams puts it this way in "Persons, Character and Morality," 13.

This eucharistic prayer captures well this summary of our journey:

> We give thanks to you, O God, for the goodness and love which
> you have made known to us in creation; in the calling of Israel to
> be your people; in your Word spoken through the prophets; and
> above all in the Word made flesh, Jesus, your Son. For in these
> last days you sent him to be incarnate from the Virgin Mary,
> to be the Savior and Redeemer of the world. In him, you have
> brought us out of error into truth, out of sin into righteousness,
> out of death into life.[3]

What remains for us in this chapter, then, is to see what more we can
say about how Christians understand the good life, and how a Christian
understanding of the good life may overlap significantly with other understandings of the good life, as well as how it may differ. We start by thinking
about *vocation,* or the calling of Christians.

8.2 CHRISTIAN VOCATION

In an opinion piece titled "The Summoned Self," *New York Times* columnist
David Brooks identifies two distinct ways of thinking about how to live one's
life.[4] The first way, the "Well-Planned Life," is represented and endorsed by
Harvard Business School Professor Clayton Christensen. To live well, according to this path, requires careful planning. First, you must work hard to
identify the purpose of your life, answering the question, "Why am I here?"
Once you have that answer, you start planning. If this is why I am here, this
is what I must do. If I think my purpose in life is to see that the hungry are
fed and the captives are set free, that should guide my decisions and priorities. How much time and energy and personal resources should I devote to
each of the many possibilities before me given my purpose? What should I
major in if I am a student? What jobs should I take? How much time can I
devote to practicing my trumpet? Should I get married or does a single life
better fit my purpose? If marriage fits, what kind of person should I marry?
You make a plan, considering all the foreseeable alternatives. You execute
the plan. You review the plan. Then, you revise the plan and start all over
again.

Brooks contrasts this ordered, controlled way of thinking about living
purposefully and well with the path that gives the title to his column, the

3. From the Episcopal Church USA *Book of Common Prayer,* Holy Eucharist, Rite
II, Eucharistic Prayer B.

4. Brooks, "Summoned Self," para. 9.

"Summoned Life." Rather than thinking of life as a well-planned project to be completed, those who take this alternative path think of life as "an unknowable landscape to be explored." We don't know enough when we are young to grasp our purpose in life and to make good plans. We don't know what is in front of us and how we or the world may change. Also, the "Well-Planned Life" seems to value too little our commitments and our relationships, things like family, friends, and place. Rather than deep introspection and careful planning, "sensitive observation" and "situational awareness" should guide one's life choices. We live responding daily to the voices and events around us.

David Brooks's conclusion, however, is surprising. Despite the column's title, he doesn't encourage us to take the second way, the "Summoned Life." Instead he concludes, "The first vision is more American. The second vision is more common elsewhere. But they are both probably useful for a person trying to live a well-considered life."

We may wonder how Christians, having shared the journey of this book, should think about this question of living one's life well, of living a good life. Brooks identifies the Harvard business professor Clayton Christensen as a serious Christian. So maybe a responsible Christian plans her life the way Christensen suggests, carefully and in detail identifying her purpose and devising a plan for achieving that purpose, and revising her plan as needed. On the other hand, in this book I've suggested that Christians should live responsively, that we are to live our lives as responses to God and to what God is doing. God calls us, summons us to follow Jesus. Jesus summons us to deny ourselves, take up our cross, and follow him (Matt 16:24). Doesn't that sound much more like the second path, the path of "calling"?

It's easy to see why the language of "calling" has been so prevalent in Christianity throughout the ages and even to the present day. The biblical story is filled with calls and callings. God called Abraham to "go from your own country and your kindred and your father's house to the land that I will show you. I will make of you a great nation, and I will bless you, and make your name great, so that you will be a blessing. . . . In you all the families of the earth shall be blessed" (Gen 12:1–3). God called to Moses out of the burning bush, telling him to go to Pharaoh and to bring the captive Israelites out of Egypt (Exod 3:1–22). God called prophets, notably Isaiah (Isa 6:1–8) and Jeremiah (Jer 1:4–19), and God called kings—David, for example (1 Sam 16:7–13). Through the angel Gabriel, God called Mary to conceive and bear a son and to name him Jesus (Luke 1:26–38). And Jesus calls to his disciples, "Come, follow me" (Matt 4:18–22).

So, in one sense, every Christian rightly believes that we all have been summoned, called by God to turn from loving the wrong things (or, perhaps, loving the right things in the wrong sort of way) and to love God with all our heart, with all our soul, with all our strength, and with all our mind, and to love our neighbors as we love ourselves (Luke 10:27). This is what Christians have sometimes called their primary vocation or calling: the calling to follow Jesus, to be his disciples wherever we go, whatever we do.

But this is a general call, a call that applies to all Christians, and, as you may have noted when thinking about the biblical calls mentioned above, sometimes God calls a particular person to a specific task or role. God speaks to Abraham, telling him to leave home. Moses hears God instruct him to go down to Egypt and tell old Pharaoh to let God's people go. This is a different type of call, a particular call, and a secondary sense of vocation. It doesn't replace or supplant the first sense, but rather directs particular Christians in living out that first sense of calling, in loving and serving God and neighbor in the particulars of their everyday lives. If the very hairs of our head are numbered (Matt 10:30; Luke 12:7), then it should be no surprise that in various ways God calls particular Christians to particular work and roles.

How Christians have understood and valued this secondary sense of vocation has varied somewhat from one historical period to the next.[5] In the medieval period, the secondary sense of vocation came to be understood as God's calling of an individual person to a specific church role as priest, or monk or nun, frequently eclipsing the primary sense of vocation. The people called by God were called to "full-time Christian ministry," and what seemed to matter above all was whether one had a church vocation as a priest or in one of the monastic orders. These were the callings about which God really cared. The church was where God and God's called ones were busy, or so many Christians not called to church work came to believe. Other work might be important for living, but not for God.

In the sixteenth century, Martin Luther and the Protestant Reformation provided a powerful corrective to this understanding of vocation as a calling only to do "religious" work, the very important work of priests and monastics. Luther had been a monk and he valued that work greatly, though he came to believe it was only different work, and not better work, than what Christians might do outside the church. In his teaching about "the priesthood of all believers," Luther argued that we each stand face to face with God and that God calls each of us daily to serve God and our neighbor, whatever we do. Church roles are different, but no more important, than

---

5. William C. Placher's *Callings* is a superb collection of readings on vocation, organized chronologically.

other jobs. Every Christian believer should, in some sense, act as a priest. Shoemakers and printers are to praise and serve God as they make shoes and print books. And in their daily work they are also somehow to serve their neighbors. Soldiers, too, can serve God, Luther argued, in his *Whether Soldiers, Too, Can Be Saved*. Whoever you are, whatever you do, you can and should do it to God's glory and to the benefit of your neighbor.

What is corrective in one era often becomes corruptive, or at least corrupted, in the next. (That may be especially true in times when clergy and others worry about treating vocation and calling as distinctively or particularly Christian ideas, rather than broader, more generic concerns.) Arguably, so it has been with vocation and Luther's expansion of calling from church roles to any institution and any role, at least in principle. The meaning of vocation as the daily work in which you serve God and your neighbor may come to mean, perhaps has come to mean, simply one's daily work, one's job, what one does to make a living. Or, if that makes vocation and calling too mundane, the mundane may be imbued with subjective value. In that case, one's calling is to the work about which you are passionate, whatever that work may be. And so, in many colleges and universities in America today, one can find special programs focused upon vocation and the discovery of what jobs, what careers one may find meaningful and purposeful.

This corrupted notion of vocation, in both of its forms, is both continuous and discontinuous with Luther's understanding. To see this, take the most frequently quoted words about vocation in the past fifty years: your vocation is "the kind of work (a) that you need most to do, and (b) that the world most needs to have done. . . . The place God calls you to is the place where your deep gladness and the world's deep hunger meet."[6] Read carefully, Frederick Buechner's account claims that a vocation *is* different from just a job. First of all, a calling needs a caller, and not merely our own passion, our own voice, albeit still and small. God does call us, Buechner helpfully reminds us.

Still, one may worry that in too much talk of vocation today, the first part of Buechner's explanation of calling, the subjective aspect, gets all the play. Buechner's rich sense of vocation may have come to mean only "Find something that you are passionate about, and go for it." That God calls us and that our vocations should be understood as responses to God's call to us and that God always calls us to turn outward and away from ourselves, to serve *others* in our vocation, to address some real need in the world, may fall out as secondary or unnecessary components of vocation, or perhaps

6. Buechner, *Wishful Thinking*, 95.

reshaped as "What the world most needs to have done is what I think the world most needs to have done" and not "the world's deep hunger."

I propose a different way of thinking about living one's life, a way different from Brooks's Well-Planned Life as well as his Summoned Life, a way informed and guided by what we have discovered about God's project, a way in which our deep gladness, if we are loving rightly and well, meets the world's genuinely deep hunger. Let's call this third way a "God-Responsive Life," for this approach encourages us to understand a good life, a well-lived life, as a life responsive to God and God's ground project and to what God is currently perceived to be doing in the world. We are called to live our lives as a response to God, to God's creative goodness, to God's care for and sustaining of the created order, to God's redemptive, transformative, and restorative activities as God aims at shalom. Our primary calling or vocation is a call to respond to God, who meets us with goodness and grace in God's created order and in Christ Jesus, who lived, died, and was raised from the dead by God, and who will come again in glory, and who in the Holy Spirit is now working in us and in the world to make all things new.

8.3 BASIC GOODS

To live a good life, as Christians understand it, is to respond to the call of God, the Creator. That is, we should live as the sorts of creatures we are created to be, to live as creations of God and as imagers of God (Gen 1:26–27) in the good world God has created. As Creator, God calls us to love things according to their real worth and to order our aims for genuinely worthy goods. Our calling is to be for the goods of God's creation.

We are in challenging territory here, so let's approach it this way. Think about someone you admire, someone you think has the right values, who understands what things are of real worth and how worthy these things are, someone who aims in his or her life for things of value, the sort of person who, you think, does as good a job at following the advice of Philippians 4:8 as anyone you know: "Finally, beloved, whatever is true, whatever is honorable, whatever is just, whatever is pure, whatever is pleasing, whatever is commendable, if there is any excellence and if there is anything worthy of praise, think about these things." And not only "think about these things"— we can be sure that the Apostle Paul also meant that we should "act on these things."

You can imagine your admirable person saying to you, "I really want to get what's going on in Thelonious Monk's 'Round Midnight'" or "I want to understand Plantinga's view of warranted belief." But you can't easily imagine that person saying, "I want to know (by counting) how many blades of grass there are on the lawns of Harvard University." You can imagine your person saying, "I'm trying to be a better mother or friend." You can't easily imagine her saying, "I'm trying to be a better liar." You can imagine your worthy person saying, "I need to visit the Rijksmuseum." You can't easily imagine him saying, "I need to make sure I've tasted every kind of marshmallow that has ever been made." You might hear her say, "It's really important to me that I commit no errors while playing infield this year." You can't imagine her saying, "I don't see what the big deal is about cutting corners at work as long as the bosses don't notice."

In reflecting upon thought experiments like this one, experiments in which we identify the sorts of things we can imagine some practically wise and admirable people pursuing, many philosophers have identified a set of "basic goods" of which the imaginable items in our paragraph above are examples, tokens, or expressions. Understanding Plantinga's view of warranted belief is worthy knowledge. No fielding errors in a softball season is a significant achievement in play. And knowledge and achievement in play are, arguably, among the basic goods. "Being for" these goods and pursuing them in some way adds meaning to our lives, makes it worth getting up in the morning, and in some respects makes life go better for us. To "be against" these goods is to fail to love and value something that is genuinely worth loving and valuing.

Surprisingly, philosophers, ordinarily not an especially agreeable bunch, have come up with quite similar lists of these basic goods worthy of our pursuit, goods valuable *for their own sake*, and not just for how we benefit from them. For example, here are four lists of basic goods of some recent philosophers:

- John Finnis: life; knowledge; play; aesthetic experience; sociability (friendship); practical reasonableness; religion[7]

- Alfonso Gómez-Lobo: life; family; friendship; work and play; experience of beauty; knowledge, both practical and theoretical; integrity of persons[8]

- James Griffin: the components of human existence [i.e., life, autonomy, and liberty]; understanding; enjoyment; deep personal relations; accomplishment[9]

---

7. Finnis, *Fundamentals of Ethics*, 50–52.

8. Gómez-Lobo, *Morality and the Human Goods*, 6–25.

9. Griffin, *Well-Being*, 67–68, and *What Can Philosophy Contribute to Ethics?*, 30.

- Timothy D. J. Chappell: life; truth, and the knowledge of the truth; friendship; aesthetic value; physical and mental health and harmony; pleasure and the avoidance of pain; reason, rationality, and reasonableness; the natural world; people; fairness; achievements; the contemplation of God (if God exists)[10]

Let's take Chappell's more expansive, though still not exhaustive, list. As Chappell suggests, life, truth, friendship, and the natural world are worth pursuing and can be valued for their own sake, and not just for how we benefit from them. It is good that these exist. We have reasons to pursue truth and knowledge, reasons to be a friend and to devote time and energy to friendships, reasons to enjoy excellent paintings and to listen attentively to Samuel Barber's *Violin Concerto Op. 14*. These things are basic goods, or tokens or examples of basic goods. They are worthy of our pursuit and of our dispositions to pursue them, to "favor [them] . . . in action, desire, emotion, or feeling"[11] because they have "to-be-pursuedness" built into them somehow, as philosopher J. L. Mackie put it.[12] Christians will explain their inherent worth, their goodness, with an appeal to God and God's creating a universe that is shot through with value. Those who are not Christians may recognize these same goods but will explain them differently, perhaps with an appeal to human nature and flourishing, while still agreeing on what the goods are.

To respond well to the Creator God thus is to recognize the goodness of God's creation and to respect the goods of creation, whatever these may be. Not everything we may want is really worthy of pursuit or worthy of the doggedness of our pursuit; we may mistakenly desire and pursue what only *appears* to be good but, in reality, is not good or is less good than it appears. (Some of my students, most mistakenly, I think, have suggested that hot original glazed Krispy Kreme donuts fall into this last class of things appearing better than they are.) On the other hand, we can also discover real goods, and we can honor their goodness in our loving them and pursuing them, and with our gratitude that they exist. To respond well to God, the Creator, thus requires us to pay attention, to study God's creation, and to recognize and value basic goods, those things that are genuinely worthy of pursuit by humans created in God's image.

Although our being for these goods does mean that we must develop dispositions to act and to desire and enjoy these goods, we are not required at every moment to pursue each and every one of these goods. That is hardly

10. Chappell, *Understanding Human Goods*, 33–65.

11. Adams, *Theory of Virtue*, 17.

12. Mackie, *Ethics*, 40.

possible. In the same way that I can believe a hot Krispy Kreme donut worthy of pursuit because of the pleasure that accompanies the act of eating the donut without also believing that I must pursue that particular pleasure at every available opportunity, so I can recognize aesthetic value, friendship, and knowledge of the truth as basic goods without being required at every moment to pursue all three. Indeed, it is not unreasonable to think that an attempt always to pursue aesthetic value, friendship, and knowledge simultaneously will often result in realizing only one good, if any, and this one at the expense of the others. How much knowledge are my friend and I likely to attain as we gaze together at an especially stunning sunset or listen attentively to John Coltrane's *Giant Steps*? How much is our enjoyment of that sunset likely to be diminished by our attending, at the same time, to either our friendship or to knowledge rather than to what Coltrane is doing? In W. Somerset Maugham's *Moon and Sixpence*, Charles Strickland, modeled on the French artist Paul Gauguin, believes he must abandon his family in order to make great achievements in his art.[13] Excellence in tennis requires a single-mindedness that precludes excellence in jazz piano, or so it may be argued. To be for these goods does not require us to pursue each of the goods at every opportunity. In many, perhaps most, cases it may be enough to be disposed to be grateful for it, should the thought of some good cross one's mind.

To be responsive to God the Creator, to live our vocations as the sorts of creatures God has created humans to be, then, requires us to identify and appreciate basic goods such as those in the lists above and to freely pursue these goods, that is, to include the pursuit of some of these goods in our projects and to value them even when they are not among our projects. But we need to clarify this last point about the goods we choose not to pursue. What if I choose to pursue achievements in work or play at the expense of a concern for what I owe to my fellow citizens? Could that be a good vocational choice? Did Charles Strickland make a good choice in abandoning his family in order to pursue better art-making?

No, I don't think so. Even though we may freely choose whether and how to pursue basic goods, recognizing the basic goods *as goods* limits or constrains what we choose and what we value. Since these are real goods, they are worthy of our respect, of our valuing and honoring them, of our loving them as the goods they are. But to violate or act against these goods is to fail to respect and value them as genuine goods. I violate a good when

13. This seems a rather common view of artists. In season 2, episode 7 of *The Marvelous Mrs. Maisel*, Declan Howell, an artist, tells Midge, "If you want to do something great, if you want to take it as far as it will go, you can't have everything. You lose family, a sense of home. But then, look at what exists."

I act against that good, when I act in ways that are incompatible with the value of a basic good. When it comes to the basic goods, I may or may not pursue one or more of these goods, but I ought never to violate, or do harm to, or fail to respect any of these goods.

Much as there are many different ways to value and pursue a basic good, so too, we can violate basic goods in different ways. Take the basic good of human life. Since life is a basic good, all things being equal, I ought not to aim at the destruction of a human life. Of course, all things are not always equal. There may be circumstances in which I am justified in harming another person, say, in self-defense, although arguably even in cases of self-defense my aim should be only protection of myself and not the death of another. In other cases, I might violate a basic good by some attitude or disposition I have toward the good. For example, I can violate the good of aesthetic experience by a habitual failure to attend to beauty and aesthetic excellence, by becoming the sort of person who doesn't care about or notice beauty. We violate basic goods by acting and feeling and loving in ways that are incompatible with the goodness of these basic goods.

A grasp of basic goods and an understanding of the different ways of *being for* the basic goods is crucial for living out our vocations well. The same is true, of course, when it comes to the many ways of violating and not being for these goods. Furthermore, since it is good for Christians to live out our calling *to be for* basic goods this gives us a reason to care that the conditions necessary for being for the basic goods, for pursuing them and favoring them in our emotions and feelings, exist not only for other Christians but for all people. If knowledge is a basic good, then it is good for all humans, whoever they are, to pursue and attain knowledge and to care about understanding and knowing what is true. If we are called to love our neighbors, and if that pursuit is not possible for those with a hungry belly and without education, or without freedom of various sorts, then we also have reasons to care for and commit ourselves to securing the goods of food, education, and freedom for others, to pursue opportunities for all *to be for* these goods.

8.4 SUFFERING AND CHRISTIAN VOCATION

The calling of the Christian is to live responsively, to respond to God, the Creator and Sustainer of a good creation, by *being for* the good as God is for the good, by our favoring basic goods in our actions, desires, loves, cares, and hopes. You may recall the two quotes that appear as the epigraph of this book. The first, from Psalm 34:8, is an encouragement to us to encounter and experience God. "Taste and see that the LORD is good." The second, from C. S. Lewis's *Problem of Pain*, reminds us that we can't get to the promised land, to living well with God and all of God's creation, without stopping at Mt. Sinai, where God declares to us in the Ten Commandments how our lives are to be responsive to God and to God's intentions for the creation.

We may need to amend Lewis's words, however, with a reference to a second mount: Golgotha, or Calvary. Perhaps we should say, "The road to the promised land runs past Sinai and through Calvary." The calling of all Christians, as we have seen, is also to respond to God who has come to us in Christ Jesus, who was crucified at Calvary, and raised from death by God. We are summoned to follow Jesus, who teaches us to love God with all our heart, all our soul, all our mind, and all our strength and to love our neighbors as ourselves. This Jesus urges us to take up our crosses and follow him.

In following Jesus, we first turn away from the world in order to see God more clearly and love God more dearly. Seeing God more clearly and loving God more dearly, we then follow Jesus back to the world that God is redeeming, transforming, and re-creating. All Christians are called to live this good life, and living this good life is to truly live, for the glory of God is for us to be fully alive.

But Jesus also tells us that to be fully alive is to die. To die to sin and our obsession with ourselves rather than others. Most of us realize that to be human is to suffer, that sorrow and suffering is part of human experience. From earth to earth, ashes to ashes, and dust to dust. Jesus does not deny that we will suffer. We bear the image of the man of dust (1 Cor 15:42–57). To be human *and* to be fully alive, calvary reminds us, is also to bear the image of Christ, the man of heaven, and to accept a second type of suffering, the suffering that comes with living a cruciform or cross-shaped life, a life of following Jesus and loving our neighbors.

We know too well the difficulties that many Christians face in living out their vocation or, at least, in living out some (mis)understandings of vocation. Take the Buechner summary of vocation as "the kind of work (a) that you need most to do, and (b) that the world most needs to have done. . . . The place God calls you to is the place where your deep gladness and the world's deep hunger meet." How many Christians can identify the work they most need to do and the work the world most needs done and also have the freedom and wherewithal to do that work? How many of us must instead simply do the work that pays the bills? How many of us can't get the work that would pay the bills?

By some estimates, somewhere between 215 and 300 million Christians living in the world today are persecuted.[14] These Christian brothers and sisters may not be free to respond to what the world most needs done. They may struggle to do the work they most need to do. We know many Christians who are ill and whose illness may prevent them from acting, from discovering what the world most needs. Many of our Christian brothers and sisters find themselves in prisons or with criminal records that will not disappear. They may not be able to do the work that they most need to do and that the world most needs to have done because no one will give them a second chance. Their need to do some work, perhaps any work, is not satisfied, and the needs of the world not fulfilled.

But this is not the whole story; there is good news, too, for the persecuted, for the sick, for the imprisoned. Although their deep gladness and the world's deep hunger may not embrace, nevertheless they can, in many and perhaps most cases, live out a different Christian vocation. They *can* live their vocations to respond to God the Creator by *being for* the good despite their tough straits. They can be grateful for the basic goods of creation and cultivate dispositions to pursue basic goods, as the opportunity permits, with others. And they can live cross-shaped lives.

They need not pursue their vocation of being for basic goods alone, by themselves. Recall the image with which chapter 7 concluded: the image of the good life of Christians as a dance of the follower of Christ with God. What follows from this image is that in being concerned with living well, Christians need better to understand our dance with God and need help in dancing better with God, help in dancing with more grace. To love God is to desire God's kingdom (Mark 1:14–15), to hope for the realization of God's ground project of shalom, and to follow Jesus in living toward the realization of that project.[15]

This image of the dance with God is, in many respects, a most helpful image for understanding our vocations. But in other ways it may be misleading, and perhaps even dangerous. One problem is that the image suggests that there are only two parties in the dance: God, who leads, and the individual who, living out her vocation, dances the dance of shalom with God. But that isn't how Christians understand themselves in relation to God or understand their vocation to be for the basic goods. There are never just two of us—me and God. There are other dancers dancing concurrently with God as well, all of us committed to following God's lead in the dance. As

14. Gomes, "ACN: Almost 300 Million Christians Persecuted," and Open Doors, "Christian Persecution."

15. See Smith, *Desiring the Kingdom*.

important as the encounter with God is, as crucial as it is that each of us engages God as a unique person, this picture is too individualistic. God meets us as individuals, face to face. But God always meets us as the persons we are, and we are always persons in community with others. And God, also, is always in community. So, Christians believe, your dance and my dance with God is part of the dance of a community, the dance of the church with God. And not only the church: since we live in a world of God's creation far larger than the church, we are part of the world's dance with God. We always dance as not only ourselves but ourselves in community, and as part of something much bigger than ourselves.

Consider, again, loving and pursuing the basic goods of creation. Most of these goods we pursue with and alongside others, as common projects. We work and play with others. In pursuing the truth and attaining knowledge, we engage in conversation and cross-examination with others. In experiencing beauty, our urge is to find someone else with whom to share our experience. We pursue the good, we are for the good, with others. As Robert Merrihew Adams writes, "Human good is found very largely in activities whose point and value depend on the participation of other people in a common project."[16] The good life for Christians is a life of friendship with God, yet not only with God but also with others who share the ground project of following Jesus, a life with others of projects *for* the goods. We must be careful not to minimize the suffering and sorrows of others, the hardships they face in pursuing their vocations. But surely it is good news that the good of friendship, of loving and being loved by others, and the good of working together on projects shared with others can be realized by all as we lead our cross-shaped lives.

Put Down the Phone: For Further Thought

1. What would you identify in Donaldina Cameron's life as the basic goods and the common projects which she seems most clearly to have pursued?

2. What do you see as the strengths and the weaknesses of the "Well-Planned Life" and of the "Summoned Life"? How is the "God-Responsive Life" similar to and different from these other views of living well?

3. Some Christians believe that God prepares us for one special someone in the world and that, in some sense, God calls us to search until we find that person. They may also think the same thing about work,

16. Adams, *Theory of Virtue*, 88.

about our jobs. What do you think of this view? Is there just one perfect person for you? One perfect job?

4. How might it be liberating to think of a job as just a job, just a way to make money, and to think that your real vocation is what you are able to do with the rest of your time having made that money? Do you think this "work to live" view leaves out something important about how Christians should view employment, or not?

5. When you look at the lists of basic human goods, are there any basic goods that you think have been overlooked? What? Are there things on these lists that you think should not be included?

6. How do you think philosophers "know" what the basic goods are? How would they explain this? How would you show that something should or shouldn't be on such a list? To what might you appeal?

7. Does the author's discussion of violating and not violating basic goods explain why killing is wrong? Looking at the lists of basic goods, can you identify other rules or principles that state what is good or right or evil or wrong given these goods?

8. What is the difference between the suffering that comes with bearing the image of a human person and the suffering that comes with bearing the image of Christ?

9. Do you think the author's criticism of one reading of Frederick Buechner's account of vocation is fair? Why or why not?

9

A CONCLUDING MUSICAL MEDITATION

There in God's Garden[1]

> Király Imre von Pécselyi (c. 1590–1641)
> trans. Erik Routley (1917–82)

There in God's garden
stands the Tree of Wisdom
whose leaves hold forth the healing of the nations:
Tree of all knowledge, Tree of all compassion,
Tree of all beauty.

Its name is Jesus,
name that says, "Our Savior!"
There on its branches see the scars of suff'ring;
see where the tendrils of our human selfhood
feed on its lifeblood.

Thorns not its own
are tangled in its foliage;
our greed has starved it, our despite has choked it.
Yet, look! It lives! Its grief has not destroyed it
nor fire consumed it.

See how its branches
reach to us in welcome;

---

1. "There in God's Garden." Words: Erik Routley © 1974 Hope Publishing Company, Carol Stream, IL 60188. All rights reserved. Used by permission.

hear what the Voice says, "Come to me, ye weary!
Give me your sickness, give me all your sorrow,
I will give blessing."

This is my ending,
this my resurrection;
into your hands, Lord, I commit my spirit.
This I have searched for; now I can possess it,
This ground is holy.

All heav'n is singing,
"Thanks to Christ whose Passion
offers in mercy healing, strength, and pardon.
Peoples and nations, take it, take it freely!"
Amen! My Master!

Together, we dance with God in worship and praise and in our work and our play. We dance to the music of our times, responding to what God is doing in sustaining the creation and in re-creating all things. There is the dance, as well, within the Godhead, a dance of Father, Son, and Holy Spirit. God, the Trinity, dances throughout eternity, dances before we join the divine dance, dances before the creation of the universe. And, as we have suggested, there is some sense in which we humans are not the only ones joining the divine dance. The whole of creation, and not humans only, is created to be responsive to God, to dance God's dance. This image of dance is helpful, but it is just one of many images that may enable us to think more clearly about our lives and how we are to engage God, one another, and the world in which we live. In closing, let's consider a new image, a new metaphor, that captures the same responsiveness of Christians to God but that shifts the emphasis to more than just the individual and God dancing together.

"In the beginning God created . . ." These words from the first chapter of the first book of the Christian Scriptures, Genesis, ring brightly and wonderfully in Christian ears. Here is God (the first chapter of the Gospel of John—"In the beginning was the Word . . ."—reminds us to think of God in three persons even here at the very beginning), a blank sheet of paper before God, as God is ready to create, ready to compose, as it were, desiring music. Magnificently and wonderfully, God creates out of nothingness a marvelously complex universe of stars and suns, planets and people, living and lifeless things. For six days God labors, and on the seventh day, at the end of it all, God sees that it is good, very good—indeed, a very good place for humans to live their lives in harmony with God and with each other and with the animals and plants and things that surround them. Each thing in creation doing what God has created it to do, each thing performing its

God-appointed task. Shalom achieved, a happy fit and flourishing for all things, it is Sabbath. God rests from creating and engages and enjoys what God has accomplished. God revels and rests in the goodness of what is.

To use only the language of creating, however, is to run the risk of thinking that, having created the world, God is more or less finished with God's work in the world. This is to risk thinking that God's work is over and done with, that God has finished all God needs to do and now the rest is up to us. To assume that God's task in the beginning is primarily that of making stuff out of nothing and, having succeeded at that, to gaze approvingly upon God's completed work is also dangerously misleading, Christians believe. If we speak only the words of creation and creative activity, we end up not with the Christian God but with the watchmaker God of the Deists, a God who creates, sets things in motion, and then sits back and rests while things go merrily (or not so merrily) on.[2] That is not the picture of God that informs the Christian understanding; that is not the God Christians discover in Christ Jesus, not the God Christians sing.

9.1 GOD AND THE SONG OF CREATION

To capture the Christian understanding of who God is and what God does as it is revealed to us in Christ, the Word of God, we need yet a different metaphor, a metaphor of constant activity, of God always engaged and involved in the created order even when God rests. The image of dance gets us close, but perhaps the image of music-making will bring us closer yet to how we should understand our activity with God. Music, because it is temporal, unlike the traditional visual arts, with a beginning, middle, and end, may be a better metaphor for getting at the dynamism of God and our lives with God.[3] So let's see what we can do with the metaphor of music.

2. Deism developed concurrently with the great strides of Newtonian science in the late seventeenth and early eighteenth centuries and offered a God who could be known without special revelation, and known *only* without special revelation. That is to say, according to the Deists, all knowledge of God comes from our observation of the workings of the world. The Deists believed that the world does, in fact, tell us that God exists and that God is good, having created a world marvelously aimed at the production of human happiness. But not all are convinced that the world as we know it is especially conducive to happiness. The French *philosophe* Denis Diderot insightfully quipped that Deists are those who have not lived long enough to become atheists.

3. The contemporary American theologian Robert W. Jenson has displayed the impressive theological credentials of the association of God and music. Jenson echoes the greatest of American theologians and philosophers, Jonathan Edwards, as he closes with the suggestion that we think of God as "a great fugue" (*Systematic Theology*, vol. 1, 236). That is a rich and interesting proposal (probably much more so to those who

How might this metaphor inform how we attempt to live good lives? How might we think of our lives as involved in the music of God, as singing and performing God's song?

A good place to begin is to think about the elements of a somewhat complex musical performance, a band or an orchestra performing some particular piece of music. Better yet, think of a jazz combo. What are the elements of a musical performance by a jazz combo? Well, of course, there are the material requirements: instruments or voices to make the sounds that will become music and the combo that uses the instruments to make the music. There must be a score, or something like a score, perhaps a chart, or merely a melody that a musician can riff. That is to say, there must be some core piece of music, whether it be a popular song or a chord chart or some melodies, something for the performer to base her performance upon.[4] But music to be performed doesn't just exist; someone must create it. For that we need a composer, an author of the music to be performed. If the music to be performed is somewhat complex, the likelihood of the musicians playing well without a leader or conductor to guide them is slim. So, let's add a leader of the musical group. We have, then, instruments and musicians, a composer, a piece of music the composer has created and a score to guide those who would perform it, and a leader, a conductor to guide skilled musicians capable of reading the score, performing the music prescribed, and following the conductor's lead.

Do we need an audience? Audiences are, usually, a good thing because performances are good events to be enjoyed—the more to hear the music, the merrier. Nevertheless, we could easily imagine a very good performance in which there would be no human audience because everyone present is a performer of the music. In that case, the audience would be none other than the performers themselves and the conductor. And we can imagine a leader and her combo perfectly content with this, for the important thing

---

better understand fugues than I). While appropriately directing us to the activity of God, I am not convinced that Jenson does justice to the activity of humans in his discussion. My image is closer to that of Edwards's himself, who described heavenly life as a "very complex tune, where respect is to be had to the proportion of a great many notes together" (quoted in Jenson, *America's Theologian*, 20). Between Edwards and Jenson lies Dietrich Bonhoeffer, who spoke of our love of God as the *cantus firmus* with which all our other loves—the contrapuntal melodies of our lives—harmonize. Bonhoeffer, *Letters and Papers from Prison*, 162–63.

4. Technically, we should distinguish between the music to be performed and the score, much as we might distinguish between the drama to be performed and the script for the drama. Roughly, the distinction is between a set of directions or guidelines a composer/author presents in order to accomplish the performance of the work she has authored, and the work she has authored. What matters is the performance; the score/script is the efficient means of accomplishing the performance.

is the performance, not the applause (or any other type of payment) of the audience. We might add, as well, that if the composer herself were a member of the combo, there would be no ears left over to hear the performance other than the "ears," perhaps, of rock, forest, and stream (a most unresponsive audience by the standards of most contemporary musicians, yet possibly more polite than many contemporary audiences!).

Now let's infuse this metaphor of music with the biblical narrative we rehearsed in our fourth chapter. When we add the biblical drama to this image of musical performance the elements look something like this:

9.1.1 God as Composer of the Music of the Universe

"In the beginning, God worked on a melody." To be sure, it doesn't have the same ring, but it does remind us of what the biblical story tells us: in creating, God had a project for the universe, a plan, a goal for how things ought to be and how things ought to go in the universe God was creating. We are reminded that God wants the universe to sing, to perform a beautiful piece, to realize shalom, the fellowship and harmony of all things with God and with one another in God. The first few chapters of Genesis tell us, as well, that God completed God's composition and, like any good composer, was eager to hear the composition performed—and was pleased with its initial performance. Why shalom? Why a creation aimed at the performance of shalom? Because shalom is good and beautiful and God loves goodness and beauty.

Think of God, then, as a master-musician, a composer well attuned to the musical gifts of all that God has created. The composer God knows what parts each bird can sing, and so writes its piece. God knows the musical abilities of the emu as well as those of the lark, and writes appropriate and fitting parts for each. (God knows, as well, the musical abilities of the dodo, and is aware of the loss of that voice, now that the dodo is extinct, and how compensation must be made for that loss in any performance without the dodo.) God knows the melody and the harmony God wants those created in God's image to perform. "Here is the world I've created and here is the music I've composed for that world. Here is the piece for the world to play, here is the harmony to be played and heard in my creation," God says. "Here is the sound that would give delight; here is the music it would be good for the universe to play. Play it excellently! Play it lovingly!" Inscribed in this piece are the parts, the roles, to be performed by each of God's created objects.

9.1.2 Shalom: The Harmony of God

Christians do not worship an unknown God. Christians believe that God has revealed to us what is good and what God's ground project is, what God is up to, what God is active in bringing about in creation. Christians profess to have gathered from the church's reading of Holy Scripture some grasp of the music God originally scored for creation and an understanding of God's desire that someday that music would be excellently performed. Indeed, Christians profess that in God's coming to us in Christ Jesus, in Christ's living and dying as a human, and in God's raising of Jesus from the dead—that is, in the incarnation, crucifixion, and resurrection of Jesus—God has guaranteed that the music of creation will be rightly and beautifully performed. God wants the universe to play and sing shalom. Shalom, the embrace of justice and peace, a life in God, the harmony of all things with God and with one another in the realization of their God-authored natures—this is the song of the spheres. This is the melody originally composed by God. This is the performance for which Christians hope. This is the music that all creation will one day sing.

So when, in Genesis 1:28, God tells humankind, created music-makers in God's image, to "be fruitful and multiply . . ." God's admonition is to fill the universe, as God has, with song. "Be in communion with God and all created things, as God is in communion with all; that is to say, sing shalom with all of your being and things will be the way they are supposed to be." Peace, justice, harmony, communion with God—that is the goal of creation.

9.1.3 The First Musicians: Adam and Eve and the Created Order

Accordingly, God created a universe capable of performing God's music and performing it excellently. Land and water, night and day, creeping things, flying things, and human beings were created to sing that song, to play God's tune. So they did sing and play, and it was good. But, as Christians interpret the book of Genesis, no sooner has God presented the score of shalom to its performers than something goes amiss. Adam and Eve wonder whether they might not write a better tune. "We need more bass, more percussion, more cowbell!!!" thinks Adam. "A little bit slower, or perhaps a little bit faster?" wonders Eve. "Not a problem," sighs the serpent, "whatever you want. Indeed, eat of this apple and you can write your own music; you won't need God for your performance."

Adam and Eve put on their headphones and begin to sing their own song, not God's, and, as the next eight or so chapters of Genesis present it, the result is extremely disheartening and depressing. When Cain sings to Abel, "Let us go out to the field" (Gen 4:8) and then kills him there, that is not God's song of shalom, that is Adam and Eve's song; that is a broken, human song. And that human song is sung again and again in the first eleven chapters of Genesis: as the "sons of God" forget their place and multiply evil in their seduction of the daughters of man (Gen 6:1–4), as Noah's children sing sin only seconds after God has delivered and blessed them (Gen 9:20–27), as men multiply bricks to build an auditorium equal to God's performance hall in the heavens (Gen 11:1–9). God's voice rings, "Be fruitful and multiply shalom." The human voice responds with song, but the song of sin, the song of harm, not shalom.

9.1.4 A New Score, A New Singer

In their reading of the first twelve chapters of Genesis, Christians are reminded that the God of Jesus Christ, the God of Israel, is a God of steadfast love, a long-suffering, ever-gracious God. The one who wants shalom for this world God has created hears the screeching of sin and wrong and determines to rescue the world, to wash the ugly music down the drain. But God will not forsake this beautiful and good creation; God first rescues the creation through Noah, only to have Noah's fruit again sing the old song of sin when the waters of the flood have receded.

God promises Abram (Gen 12:3) that God will create from Abram's children a great nation to be a blessing to all people, to all things. The narrative of the Old Testament is the story of Israel, the people through whom God acts to bless all nations, a nation of singers created by God to perform God's music. Sometimes Israel sings God's song. Sometimes Israel finds herself in a foreign land, by the waters of Babylon, unable to sing the songs of Zion. God remains ever faithful to Israel; God never forgets the promise to bless Israel and to bless all the nations through Israel. Finally, that blessing of God upon all peoples is made manifest in the fruit of Israel, Jesus of Nazareth.

Christians see in Jesus one who tells us anew of the faithful Creator who wishes to dance and sing with us, wishes for harmony, and one who is now active, making that harmony possible again, and enlists us in this work. In the midst of ugly noise, Jesus sings shalom, takes our sin-strained voices as his own, having offered his voice to God for our sakes. He is singer; he is song, God's song of shalom sung for us, and silenced, but raised again from silent death to sing with Father and Spirit forever.

9.1.5 New Song, New Singers, Old Voices

The Christian belief, then, is that God has been involved in the universe from creation onward, working to accomplish the performance of the music God has written for the universe, that dream of mystic sweet communion of God with all that is. In one sense that work of God is completed or finalized by the death and resurrection of Jesus Christ—God has completed writing the melody of the universe. And God's raising of Jesus from death is a guarantee that the music of shalom will someday ring the spheres. In another sense, however, right now we await that singing, the universal recognition of the victory of God in Jesus; the music has not yet been performed and cannot be fully performed until all things are made new by God. We stand, now, in between times: after the time that God has come in Christ to make that performance possible, yet before the time of the completely realized performance of shalom. We live in a time of rehearsal. The performance will take place; this is our hope. Christ has secured this. But we are not yet ready for that performance. All things are being made new, but all is not yet made new. We must think of two performances—a performance that only "approximates" shalom, a best-we-can-do-given-our-current-conditions performance, and a final (although unending) performance of shalom, a "realization" of shalom, God's grand ground project.

In the meantime, before the realized performance, for this in-between time, God has created a new community to lead in singing God's song. God calls into being a community, like Israel before God's incarnation in Jesus, to be a blessing to all nations by singing the song of God. That new community, the church, is the body of musicians, like Israel entrusted with the task of discovering the score, reading the melody, discerning the conductor's lead, and singing and playing God's song now and until that day when all creation will fully and finally sing God's song. That is our vocation. That is our living well, a good life.

A qualification must immediately be added. The church is the combo, or the choir, to perform God's music *as well as it can be performed in the present age prior to the singing of the new creation, to perform God's music as God wants the music performed in this in-between time.* The church is appointed by God to sing God's song, but to sing a song they cannot yet fully sing because of the presence of sin and evil in the world, a song that the world cannot fully and truly hear and perform with us until the new creation. The resurrection of Christ promises new eyes to see God's score and new lips with which to sing. But our sight is only slowly restored, our voices are only gradually improving, as we move only slightly, perhaps, toward the promised concert of shalom.

And now, a second qualification. The leader or conductor, aware that the performance conditions for rehearsals are not identical with the performance conditions for the final performance of the music, may conduct a different music, may call for roles appropriate for current conditions, may require music responsive to other fledgling performers, rather than the perfectly harmonious music of shalom. And this is to say that the musicians must not only know the score, but they must always follow the leader, aware that they are not yet ready to perform as they someday will, aware that they are being prepared to perform, and aware that their performance, even now, is of the greatest import as they follow the conductor's lead in playing well a music that honors the Composer of all things and all that God has created.

9.2 CHRISTIAN REFLECTION AND THE MUSIC OF GOD

We have been trying to grasp how Christians understand living well, what Christians understand the good life to be. First of all, as we have seen, the God-responsive life is a communal life. The Christian response to God is always the response of an individual, but always the response of an individual-in-community, of one mindful of her relation to others, of an individual who is *both* an individual performer and part of an ensemble. What matters, finally, is a loving performance of beautiful music, the performance God desires, and although there may well be solo bits as part of that performance, and much room for improvisation, those solo bits occur before or after or in between the music of an ensemble and are meant to be heard in relation to the music of the entire ensemble. We play together, as part of a combo, even when we are playing solo. Our music is richer, deeper, and more sonorous because we play together with others.

Although Christians are, essentially, members of the church, always first and foremost connected with that body of those who have recognized God's call to them and seek to respond fittingly to God's call, Christian identity is not only corporate. Christians live as individuals as well as members of the body of Christ. Christians live, too, in the world, although they are not of the world. To be Christian, to be a member of the church, is to seek to discern through conversation and study with other members not only what God calls the church to do here and now but also God's call to the world and to oneself. What am I to do? Who am I to be? What am I to do with this melody? These questions are answered in conversation with the church, the visible body of Christ.

Christians believe that together they are called to be a particular community of performance, called to be a blessing to all as they respond to God's acting in the world and as they prepare to play shalom. Theologian Helmut Thielicke once wrote about theology, "Insofar as we are determined to be true theologians, we think within the community of God's people, and for that community, and in the name of that community."[5] So it should be as Christians think about the good life and living well. The church and her members are attempting to discern what sort of people they should be, what music they should perform, in the light of God's final aims for creation and in the light of God's current activity in the world. Thinking about what we should value, what we should love and how much we should love, is the church's work, is a discipline whose goal is to enable the church and the people of the church to live faithfully and well, to play the music God is conducting for this particular moment, the music God is now directing the church to play, as well as to prepare to perform the final song of shalom.

Many find this disconcerting. It is one thing for me to speak for myself about what I take to be fitting and good. But what authority do I have to speak for the church, the body of Christ? Only the authority of one who, as the great twentieth-century theologian Karl Barth wrote, "in all humility . . . was willing to risk being such a Church in his own place and as well as he knew how."[6] The Christian thinker who attempts to articulate an appropriate Christian understanding or view of living well, of basic human goods and the good life, speaks *to* and *for* the church because she understands herself as part of that body seeking to be faithful to the risen Lord.

Christian reflection upon living well is theo-centric. The goal of Christian thought about the good life is not, ultimately, to discover the means to happiness or human flourishing, although some Christians may believe that happiness and human flourishing are constituted by our living faithfully. The earth, however, is the Lord's. The creator of the universe is the author of the song Christians hope to sing. As such, the story of the universe is God's story, not (or not first of all) ours. Our focus should be upon God and God's projects, not our story and our projects. It is God's story, God's song, that Christians seek to discern and sing, responding not only to God the composer but also to God the conductor, confident that the conductor will fittingly guide their performance at this time and in this place.

Christian reflection is Trinitarian in its theo-centricity. God is always Father, Son, and Holy Spirit. Christian music arises in the recognition that God is good, the composer of the music that we are to perform, but God's

---

5. Thielicke, *Little Exercise for Young Theologians*, 4.
6. Quoted in Meilaender, *Bioethics*, xiii.

role does not end there. In Christ, God is leader and conductor, as well as composer, of that song. Without the song of Christ, we could not know rightly and well the music God would have us perform. Absent the song of Christ, we could not hope to perform well. In the Holy Spirit, God aids and assists our preparation and our performance of God's music. Without the singing of Christ and the harmony of the Holy Spirit, we could not now or in the future perform God's melody as we should. We are enabled and empowered by the Spirit in witness to the Christ who has come to us from God the Father.

9.3 HOW CAN WE KEEP FROM SINGING?

This chapter opened with a profound hymn text of a seventeenth-century Hungarian (translated by the English hymnologist Erik Routley and set to music by K. Lee Scott, a contemporary American composer). It is a wonderful poem for the Easter season, first telling the story of Jesus, the Tree of wisdom, tree of all knowledge, all compassion, and all beauty, offering hope and healing to the creation. But this tree is also a tree of suffering brought on by human sin. Our wrongdoing, our rejection of God's project, has added thorns and has threatened the very life of the tree. Despite his suffering, the open arms of Jesus, the Tree of Life, reach out to all. The singer of the hymn, having grasped this story of the Tree, locates her own story in the story of Jesus. Thus, she rests, at last, in the holy ground of the tree. Things do not stop there. The hymn reaches its goal, its ending, when the singer's voice joins the song of heaven, inviting all nations and peoples to the tree of life that brings healing and restoration. A wonderful song indeed! A song, Christians believe, fully alive, we shall someday sing.

BIBLIOGRAPHY

Adams, Robert Merrihew. *A Theory of Virtue: Excellence in Being for the Good*. Oxford: Clarendon, 2006.

Aristotle. *Nicomachean Ethics*. Translated with introduction, notes and glossary by Terence Irwin. 2nd ed. Indianapolis: Hackett, 1999.

Augustine. *Confessions*. Translated with an introduction and notes by Henry Chadwick. Oxford World's Classics. New York: Oxford University Press, 2009.

Barth, Karl. *Church Dogmatics*. Vol. IV/1, *The Doctrine of Reconciliation*. Edinburgh: T&T Clark, 1956.

Batson, C. Daniel. *Altruism in Humans*. New York: Oxford University Press, 2011.

Benedict XVI. "Angelus: St. Peter's Square, Sunday 22 October 2006." https://w2.vatican.va/content/benedict-xvi/en/angelus/2006/documents/hf_ben-xvi_ang_20061022.html.

Bonhoeffer, Dietrich. *Letters and Papers from Prison*. Edited by Eberhard Bethge. New York: Macmillan, 1967.

———. *A Testament to Freedom: The Essential Writings of Dietrich Bonhoeffer*. Edited by Geffrey B. Kelly and F. Burton Nelson. Rev. ed. San Francisco: HarperSanFrancisco, 1995.

———. *Theological Education Underground, 1937–1940*. Edited by Victoria J. Barnett. Translated by Victoria J. Barnett et al. Dietrich Bonhoeffer Works 15. Minneapolis: Fortress, 2012.

Boulton, Wayne G., Thomas D. Kennedy, and Allen Verhey, eds. *From Christ to the World: Introductory Readings in Christian Ethics*. Grand Rapids: Eerdmans, 1994.

Bradley, F. H. *Ethical Studies*. London: Oxford University Press, 1962.

Brooks, David. "The Summoned Self." *The New York Times*, August 2, 2010, A23. https://www.nytimes.com/2010/08/03/opinion/03brooks.html.

Buechner, Frederick. *Wishful Thinking: A Theological ABC*. New York: Harper & Row, 1973.

Chappell, Timothy D. J. *Understanding Human Goods: A Theory of Ethics*. Edinburgh: Edinburgh University Press, 1998.

Charities Aid Foundation. "CAF World Giving Index 2018: A Global View of Generosity." October 2018. https://www.givingtuesday.org/lab/2018/10/caf-world-giving-index-2018.

Chesterton, G. K. *The Father Brown Omnibus*. New York: Dodd, Mead, 1951.

Creedon, Jeremiah. "God with a Million Faces." *The Utne Reader*, July-August 1998. https://www.utne.com/community/godwithamillionfaces.

Descartes, René. *Meditations on First Philosophy: with Selections from the Objections and Replies*. Translated by Michael Moriarty. Oxford World's Classics. New York: Oxford University Press, 2008.

DeYoung, Rebecca Konyndyk. *Vainglory: The Forgotten Vice*. Grand Rapids: Eerdmans, 2014.

Edwards, Jonathan. *The Nature of True Virtue*. In *Ethical Writings*, edited by Paul Ramsey, 539–627. Works of Jonathan Edwards 8. New Haven: Yale University Press, 1989.

———. "Personal Narrative." In *Letters and Personal Writings*, edited by George S. Claghorn, 791–804. Works of Jonathan Edwards 16. New Haven: Yale University Press, 1998.

———. "The 'Spider' Letter." In *Scientific and Philosophical Writings*, edited by Wallace E. Anderson, 151–53. Works of Jonathan Edwards 6. New Haven: Yale University Press, 1980.

Episcopal Church U.S.A. *The Book of Common Prayer*. New York: Church Publishing, 1979.

Finnis, John. *Fundamentals of Ethics*. Washington, DC: Georgetown University Press, 1983.

Francis, Pope. *Laudato Si'*. May 24, 2015. http://w2.vatican.va/content/francesco/en/encyclicals/documents/papa-francesco_20150524_enciclica-laudato-si.html.

———. "Letter of His Holiness Pope Francis according to which an Indulgence Is Granted to the Faithful on the Occasion of the Extraordinary Jubilee of Mercy." http://w2.vatican.va/content/francesco/en/letters/2015/documents/papa-francesco_20150901_lettera-indulgenza-giubileo-misericordia.html.

Gomes, Robin. "ACN: Almost 300 Million Christians Persecuted." *Vatican News*, November 23, 2018. https://www.vaticannews.va/en/church/news/2018–11/can-religious-persecution-christians-report.html.

Gómez-Lobo, Alfonso. *Morality and the Human Goods*. Washington, DC: Georgetown University Press, 2002.

Griffin, James. *Well-Being: Its Meaning, Measurement, and Moral Importance*. Oxford: Clarendon, 1986.

———. *What Can Philosophy Contribute to Ethics?* Oxford: Oxford University Press, 2015.

Haidt, Jonathan. *The Righteous Mind: Why Good People Are Divided by Politics and Religion*. New York: Vintage, 2012.

Hauerwas, Stanley, and Samuel Wells, eds. *The Blackwell Companion to Christian Ethics*. Oxford: Blackwell, 2004.

Hays, Richard. *The Moral Vision of the New Testament: A Contemporary Introduction to New Testament Ethics*. San Francisco: HarperOne, 1996.

Hill, Thomas E., Jr. "Servility and Self-Respect." In *Autonomy and Self-Respect*, 4–18. Cambridge: Cambridge University Press, 1991.

Irenaeus. *Against Heresies*. Translated by Alexander Roberts and William Rambaut. In vol. 1 of *The Ante-Nicene Fathers*, edited by Alexander Roberts and James Donaldson. Buffalo, NY: Christian Literature, 1885. Revised and edited for New Advent by Kevin Knight. http://www.newadvent.org/fathers/0103.htm.

James, William. *The Varieties of Religious Experience: A Study in Human Nature.* New York: Penguin, 1982.

Jenson, Robert W. *America's Theologian: A Recommendation of Jonathan Edwards.* Oxford: Oxford University Press, 1988.

———. *Systematic Theology.* Vol. 1, *The Triune God.* Oxford: Oxford University Press, 1997.

Keillor, Garrison. *Wobegon Boy.* New York: Penguin, 1997.

Kelly, Geffrey B., and F. Burton Nelson. "Editors' Introduction: Solidarity with the Oppressed; Bonhoeffer the Man." In *A Testament to Freedom: The Essential Writings of Dietrich Bonhoeffer,* edited by Geffrey B. Kelly and F. Burton Nelson, 3–46. New York: HarperCollins, 1990.

Kennedy, Thomas D. "Habit's Harsh Bondage." *Christian Reflection,* vol. 5, The Pornographic Culture (2002) 31–37.

Kierkegarrd, Søren. *Fear and Trembling.* Translated by Alastair Hannay. Penguin Classics. New York: Penguin, 1986.

King, Martin Luther, Jr. "Address at the Conclusion of the Selma to Montgomery March, March 25, 1965." https://kinginstitute.stanford.edu/king-papers/documents/address-conclusion-selma-montgomery-march.

———. "Letter from a Birmingham Jail." In *From Christ to the World: Introductory Readings in Christian Ethics,* edited by Wayne G. Boulton, Thomas D. Kennedy, and Allen Verhey, 427–36. Grand Rapids: Eerdmans, 1994.

Kirk, Kenneth E. *The Vision of God: The Christian Doctrine of the Summum Bonum.* 1931. Reprint, Harrisburg, PA: Morehouse, 1991.

Lewis, C.S. *The Four Loves.* New York: HarperOne, 2017.

———. *Mere Christianity.* New York: HarperOne, 2012.

———. *A Preface to Paradise Lost.* Oxford: Oxford University Press, 1961.

———. *The Problem of Pain.* New York: HarperOne, 2015.

MacIntyre, Alasdair. *After Virtue.* 2nd ed. Notre Dame: University of Notre Dame Press, 1984.

———. *Ethics in the Conflicts of Modernity: An Essay on Desire, Practical Reasoning, and Narrative.* Cambridge: Cambridge University Press, 2016.

Mackie, J. L. *Ethics: Inventing Right and Wrong.* New York: Penguin, 1977.

Martin, Mildred Crowl. *Chinatown's Angry Angel: The Story of Donaldina Cameron.* Palo Alto, CA: Pacific Books, 1977.

Maugham, W. Somerset. *The Moon and Sixpence.* New York: Vintage Classics, 2009.

Meilaender, Gilbert. *Bioethics: A Primer for Christians.* 2nd ed. Grand Rapids: Eerdmans. 2005.

Merton, Thomas. *Thoughts in Solitude.* New York: Farrar, Straus and Giroux, 1999.

Miller, Christian B. *The Character Gap: How Good Are We?* New York: Oxford University Press, 2018.

Moskos, Peter. *In Defense of Flogging.* New York: Basic Books, 2011.

Mouw, Richard J. *Political Evangelism.* Grand Rapids: Eerdmans, 1974.

Murdoch, Iris. *The Sovereignty of the Good.* London: Ark, 1985.

Nagel, Thomas. "Moral Luck." In *Mortal Questions,* 24–38. Cambridge: Cambridge University Press, 1979.

Niebuhr, H. Richard. *The Kingdom of God in America.* New York: Harper & Row, 1959.

———. *The Responsible Self: An Essay in Christian Moral Philosophy.* New York: Harper & Row, 1963.

Niebuhr, Reinhold. *The Nature and Destiny of Man: A Christian Interpretation.* Vol. 1, *Human Nature.* New York: Scribner's, 1964.

O'Donovan, Oliver. *Self, World, and Time: An Induction.* Ethics as Theology 1. Grand Rapids: Eerdmans, 2013.

Open Doors. "Christian Persecution in Focus." https://www.opendoorsusa.org/christian-persecution/.

Pascal, Blaise. *Pensées.* Translated by A. J. Krailsheimer. New York: Penguin, 1966.

Pentin, Edward. "Pope: 'How I Wish for a Church That Is Poor and for the Poor!'" *National Catholic Register,* March 16, 2013. http://www.ncregister.com/blog/edward-pentin/pope-how-i-wish-for-a-church-that-is-poor-and-for-the-poor.

Placher, William C., ed. *Callings: Twenty Centuries of Christian Wisdom on Vocation.* Grand Rapids: Eerdmans, 2005.

Plantinga, Cornelius, Jr. *Not the Way It's Supposed to Be: A Breviary of Sin.* Grand Rapids: Eerdmans, 2013.

Plato. *Defence of Socrates, Euthyphro, Crito.* Translated by David Gallop. Oxford World's Classics. New York: Oxford University Press, 2008.

———. *Phaedo.* Translated by David Gallop. Oxford World's Classics. New York: Oxford University Press, 2009.

———. *Timaeus and Critias.* Translated by Robin Waterfield. Oxford World's Classics. New York: Oxford University Press, 2009.

Prothero, Stephen. *God Is Not One: The Eight Rival Religions That Run the World—and Why Their Differences Matter.* New York: HarperOne, 2010.

Roberts, Robert C. "Forgivingness." *American Philosophical Quarterly* 32 (1995) 289–306.

Sledge, Benjamin. "Why I'm a Christian (and Continue to Suck at Being One)." *Heartsupport.* https://blog.heartsupport.com/why-im-a-christian-and-continue-to-suck-at-being-one-5d7cb730e3a2.

Smith, Christian. *Souls in Transition: The Religious and Spiritual Lives of Emerging Adults.* New York: Oxford University Press, 2009.

Smith, James K. A. *Desiring the Kingdom: Worship, Worldview, and Cultural Formation.* Grand Rapids: Baker Academic, 2009.

———. *You Are What You Love.* Grand Rapids: Brazos, 2016.

Sookhdeo, Patrick. "Mission and Conversion in Pakistan." In *The Terrible Alternative: Christian Martyrdom in the Twentieth Century,* edited by Andrew Chandler, 102–18. New York: Cassell, 1998.

Taylor, Charles. *Sources of the Self: The Making of Modern Identity.* Cambridge: Harvard University Press, 1989.

Thielicke, Helmut. *A Little Exercise for Young Theologians.* Translated by Charles L. Taylor. Grand Rapids: Eerdmans, 1962.

Thompson, Francis. *The Hound of Heaven and Other Poems.* Wesley, MA: Branden, 2000.

Tolstoy, Leo. *The Death of Ivan Ilych and Other Stories.* Translated by Ayler Maude and J. D. Duff. New York: Signet Classics, 2012.

White, Janet Ballantyne. *Esther: Story of a Pakistani Girl.* N.p.: 1960.

Williams, Bernard. "Persons, Character and Morality." In *Moral Luck: Philosophical Papers, 1973–1980,* 1–19. Cambridge: Cambridge University Press, 1981.

Wills, Garry. *Saint Augustine's Childhood: Confessiones Book One.* New York: Viking, 2001.

Wolf, Susan. *Meaning in Life and Why It Matters*. Princeton: Princeton University Press, 2010.

Wolterstorff, Nicholas. "For Justice in Shalom." In *From Christ to the World: Introductory Readings in Christian Ethics*, edited by Wayne G. Boulton, Thomas D. Kennedy, and Allen Verhey, 251–53. Grand Rapids: Eerdmans, 1994.

———. *In This World of Wonders: Memoir of a Life in Learning*. Grand Rapids: Eerdmans, 2019.

Wong, Kristin, and Kathryn Wong. *Fierce Compassion: The Life of Abolitionist Donaldina Cameron*. Saline, MI: New Earth Enterprises, 2012.

Wuthnow, Robert. *After Heaven: Spirituality in America since the 1950s*. Berkeley: University of California Press, 1999.

Yancey, Philip. *Rumors of Another World: What on Earth Are We Missing?* Grand Rapids: Zondervan, 2003.

Zagzebski, Linda. "Religious Luck." *Faith and Philosophy* 11 (1994) 397–413.

INDEX OF SCRIPTURAL REFERENCES

INDEX OF SUBJECTS

CPSIA information can be obtained
at www.ICGtesting.com
Printed in the USA
LVHW111306070120
642784LV00002B/288/P